P9-DVK-147

Daily doses of God's Word gave me the strength, wisdom, and courage I needed to face each day as I lost my husband to Alzheimer's disease. In *Grace for the Unexpected Journey*, Debbie Barr weaves together practical advice with biblical truths to inspire, uplift, and encourage those who have the heartbreaking responsibility of caring for a loved one with dementia.

KIM CAMPBELL, *wife of Glen Campbell; founder of CareLiving.org*

As our population continues to age, we are increasingly faced with challenges like Alzheimer's and those who suffer from it—either because they themselves have this debilitating disease or because they are caring for someone who does. All too often this journey leads caregivers to feelings of isolation, inadequacy, frustration, and grief. Debbie Barr's devotional can change this part of the journey by giving permission to slow down and be authentic with ourselves and with those around us. More than that, it gives us the space to be real with God as we cry out in anguish. Instead of offering simple answers, this devotional validates the pain we face while still offering hope. I encourage anyone caring for someone with cognitive decline to open this book and find fresh air.

HEATH GREENE, *clinical licensed psychologist; executive director, Associates in Christian Counseling; assistant teaching professor, Wake Forest University*

GRACE

FOR THE
UNEXPECTED
JOURNEY

*A 60-Day Devotional for Alzheimer's
and Other Dementia Caregivers*

DEBORAH BARR

MOODY PUBLISHERS
CHICAGO

© 2018 by
DEBORAH BARR

All rights reserved. No part of this book may be reproduced in any form without permission in writing from the publisher, except in the case of brief quotations embodied in critical articles or reviews.

All Scripture quotations, unless otherwise indicated, are taken from the *Holy Bible, New Living Translation*, copyright © 1996, 2004, 2007, 2013, 2015. Used by permission of Tyndale House Publishers, Inc., Carol Stream, Illinois 60188, U.S.A. All rights reserved.

Scripture quotations marked NIV are taken from the Holy Bible, New International Version®, NIV®. Copyright © 1973, 1978, 1984, 2011 by Biblica, Inc.™ Used by permission. All rights reserved worldwide. www.zondervan.com. The "NIV" and "New International Version" are trademarks registered in the United States Patent and Trademark Office by Biblica, Inc.™

Scripture quotations marked ESV are from The Holy Bible, English Standard Version® (ESV®), copyright © 2001 by Crossway, a publishing ministry of Good News Publishers. Used by permission. All rights reserved.

Scripture quotations marked TLB are taken from *The Living Bible* copyright © 1971. Used by permission of Tyndale House Publishers, Inc., Carol Stream, Illinois 60188. All rights reserved.

Scripture quotations marked CSB® are taken from the Christian Standard Bible®, Copyright © 2017 by Holman Bible Publishers. Used by permission. Christian Standard Bible®, and CSB® are federally registered trademarks of Holman Bible Publishers.

Scripture quotations marked AMP are taken from the Amplified® Bible, Copyright © 2015 by The Lockman Foundation. Used by permission. www.Lockman.org

Scripture quotations marked NKJV are taken from the *New King James Version®*. Copyright © 1982 by Thomas Nelson, Inc. Used by permission. All rights reserved.

Emphasis to Scripture has been added by the author.

Some names and details have been changed to protect the privacy of individuals.

Edited by Elizabeth Cody Newenhuyse
Cover and interior design: Erik M. Peterson
Cover image: Image 265836 / Stocksy United Photography

Library of Congress Cataloging-in-Publication Data
Names: Barr, Deborah, author.
Title: Grace for the unexpected journey : a 60-day devotional for Alzheimer's and other dementia caregivers / Deborah Barr.
Description: Chicago : Moody Publishers, 2018. | Includes bibliographical references.
Identifiers: LCCN 2017040147 (print) | LCCN 2017045307 (ebook) | ISBN 9780802496331 ISBN 9780802416780
Subjects: LCSH: Caregivers--Prayers and devotions. | Alzheimer's disease--Religious aspects--Christianity. | Dementia--Religious aspects--Christianity.
Classification: LCC BV4910.9 (ebook) | LCC BV4910.9 .B36 2018 (print) | DDC 242/.4--dc23
LC record available at https://lccn.loc.gov/2017040147

We hope you enjoy this book from Moody Publishers. Our goal is to provide high-quality, thought-provoking books and products that connect truth to your real needs and challenges. For more information on other books and products focusing on your most important relationships from a biblical perspective, go to www.moodypublishers.com or write to:

Moody Publishers
820 N. LaSalle Boulevard
Chicago, IL 60610

1 3 5 7 9 10 8 6 4 2

Printed in the United States of America

To Dwight Harris

Contents

Foreword

Walking with my mother on the dementia journey has given me a deep empathy for caregivers. To watch the unraveling of the tapestry that was once the picture of life, health, and vitality is painful. The photo is now marred with dark blotches and tattered memories. I remember the sadness I felt as I watched Mom's memory fade. However, it was my own memories of how she cared for me when I was young and how we shared life together as adults that gave me the will to keep walking with her to the end of the road.

In more recent years I have had the opportunity to attend support groups for those who are caring for spouses who have Alzheimer's disease. As I have listened to the stories of others, I have been reminded of the mixed thoughts and emotions of loneliness, sadness, frustration, hopelessness, and wondering, "Can I endure?" I have also been encouraged by the unconditional love and devotion of those who walk with someone who has a form of dementia.

I have also observed how often these caregivers spoke of their faith in God, and how God gave peace, strength, and the will to keep walking. One wife said, "I don't think I could make it without God and my church family." Another said, "This is the hardest thing I have ever done, but I know that God will see me through." A husband said, "I love my wife, and it hurts to lose her day by day, but God is with me. I could not make it without Him."

I have known Debbie Barr for more than thirty years. When she told me that she wanted to write a devotional book for caregivers of those with Alzheimer's and other types of dementia, I was excited. She, Dr. Ed Shaw, and I had earlier written the book *Keeping Love Alive as Memories Fade: The 5 Love Languages and the Alzheimer's Journey*. Debbie's deep concern and compassion for dementia caregivers is rooted in the heartfelt stories they told as she interviewed them for that book and spent time with them in support groups. As this book attests, she has a genuine love for those who walk the sometimes lonely road of caring for a spouse or parent with dementia.

As I have read these devotionals, I have found them insightful and encouraging. I believe you too will find them a welcome voice reminding you of the One who promised, "Lo, I am with you always, even to the end of the age."

GARY D. CHAPMAN, PhD
Author of *The 5 Love Languages*

What's Different About This Devotional Book?

As a dementia caregiver, you face both spiritual and practical challenges that others do not face. *Grace for the Unexpected Journey* is different from other daily devotionals because it was written with these unique caregiving challenges in mind. Each daily entry focuses on a spiritual or practical challenge commonly faced by dementia caregivers.

As you read each day's devotional, open your heart and mind to God as you ponder the message and meditate on its key Scripture verse. If you wish, respond to the optional thought questions and/or keep an ongoing journal in the space provided. Day by day, as you do any or all of these things, it is my prayer that you will be encouraged to lean more fully on God and draw strength from His empowering Word.

May God richly and graciously bless you as you walk the unexpected journey with Him!

DEBBIE BARR
WINSTON-SALEM, NC

Who Is a Caregiver?

Any person who provides direct care to someone with Alzheimer's disease or another kind of dementia is a *caregiver*. Typically, caregivers are family members. Most often, the spouse or an adult son or daughter serves as the primary caregiver. In countries other than the United States and Canada, this person may be called a *carer* or *caretaker*.

Throughout this devotional, *care partner* is sometimes used instead of *caregiver*. When dementia is in the early stages, *care partner* is an appropriate term because it places the person with the disease on equal footing with the person providing care; they are *partners*. This term is also fitting because family care partners tend to provide care with a sense of loyalty that aligns with the definition of *partner*: "a player on the same side or team as another" (dictionary.com). As dementia progresses, care partnering gradually transitions to a more truly care *giving* role. At any point in the disease, however, the term caregiver is correct, whether the person providing care is a member of the family, an unpaid volunteer, or a paid professional.

The Words of God

*The rain and snow come down from the heavens
and stay on the ground to water the earth.
They cause the grain to grow,
producing seed for the farmer
and bread for the hungry.
It is the same with my word.
I send it out, and it always produces fruit.
It will accomplish all I want it to,
and it will prosper everywhere I send it.*

ISAIAH 55:10–11

The days of our lives are like fingerprints: no two are exactly alike.

Each day unfolds in its own unique way. Every day, the things around us change. Today's weather, news stories, and to-do lists will be different than yesterday's. We are constantly changing too. Emotionally, physically, and spiritually, we are not the same today as we were yesterday or last week or a decade ago. Some days we wake refreshed; other days, unrested. Some days the glass may seem half-full; other days, half-empty. Friends, family members, and others weave in and out of our lives as the months and years go by.

For us, nothing stays exactly the same as each day turns into another. It's the opposite with God. He is always exactly the same—yesterday, today, tomorrow, and forever.[1] God's complete knowledge of us never changes either. He knows exactly "where we are coming from" today, just as He knows what our attitudes and concerns will be tomorrow.

As you embark on this 60-day devotional journey, you can both rest in and rejoice in God's perfect knowledge of you and of every unique day of your life. While the daily commentaries are just human thoughts and reflections upon the words of God, the *Word of God*—the Scripture verses themselves—can make happen in your life the things that God wants for you. The words of God do not return to Him void.

What might God want His words to accomplish in your life? As you meet with Him daily, you can do so with a sense of anticipation—because God promises that His words "will accomplish all I want it to."

What might God want His words
to accomplish in your life?

REFLECTIONS ON *THE WORDS OF GOD*

According to Isaiah 55:10–11, how powerful are the
words of God?

How do you think these verses apply to you while you
are on the caregiving journey?

My journal . . .

The Unexpected Journey

By faith Abraham obeyed when he was called to go out to a place that he was to receive as an inheritance. And he went out, not knowing where he was going.

HEBREWS 11:8 (ESV)

Are you surprised to find yourself in a caregiving role at this stage of your life? Did you have other plans in mind? Of course you did! Yet, here you are, on the unexpected journey, perhaps still chafing at the assignment the Lord has given you, and full of questions.

Lettie Burd Cowman likely once felt as you do right now. She and her husband were pioneer missionaries in Japan from 1901 until 1917. When Lettie's husband, Charles, became ill they reluctantly returned to California. For the next six years Lettie was Charles's devoted care partner.

Disappointed, heartbroken, and seeking encouragement for herself and Charles, Lettie began to cobble together a book consisting of sermon excerpts, poems, and writings by the Christian leaders of her time. Interspersed among this compilation are paragraphs presumably written by Lettie herself. Following commentary about Abraham, who embarked on a journey without knowing his destination, Lettie wrote:

> *It is by no means enough to set out cheerfully with your God on any venture of faith. Tear into the smallest pieces any itinerary for the journey which your imagination may have drawn up.*
>
> *Nothing will fall out as you expect.*
>
> *Your guide will keep to no beaten path. He will lead you by a way such as you have never dreamed your eyes would look upon. He knows no fear, and He expects you to fear nothing while He is with you.*[1]

Although Lettie's words were written more than a hundred years ago, they remain an apt description of any unexpected journey of faith—such as the caregiving journey upon which you have already embarked. Like Abraham, caregivers step into the future with no itinerary and no map for the journey ahead.

Abraham trusted God and was spectacularly rewarded for his faith: God called him His friend.[2] As a believing caregiver, it is your privilege to now fully rely upon Jesus, the "friend who sticks closer than a brother."[3] He walks this unexpected journey of faith with you.

Like Abraham, caregivers step into the future with no itinerary and no map for the journey ahead.

REFLECTIONS ON *THE UNEXPECTED JOURNEY*

Circle the emotions below that you have experienced on your unexpected journey so far.[*]

SHOCK	NUMBNESS	DENIAL
DISBELIEF	DISORGANIZATION	CONFUSION
SEARCHING	YEARNING	GOING CRAZY
ANXIETY	PANIC	FEAR
ANGER	HATE	BLAME (SELF, OTHERS)
TERROR	RESENTMENT	RAGE
JEALOUSY	GUILT	REGRET
SADNESS	DEPRESSION	LONELINESS
EMPTINESS	HELPLESS	FRUSTRATION
LOW SELF-ESTEEM	OUT OF CONTROL	MISSING HIM/HER
RELIEF	DESPAIR	BITTERNESS
EMBARRASSMENT	IRRITABILITY	ENVY

[*] List excerpted from unpublished caregiver support group curriculum by Edward G. Shaw, MD, MA.

As you were reading Lettie Cowman's description of a "faith venture" in the light of your own caregiving journey, did you feel more anticipation or more apprehension?

Express your anticipation or apprehension, along with the emotions you circled in the chart, to God in prayer, either spoken or written below.

My journal . . .

Day 3

Caregiver School

Behold, God is exalted in his power;
who is a teacher like him?

JOB 36:22 (ESV)

At first glance, it seems that caregiving is all about meeting the needs of the person with dementia. In fact, there is a purpose for you, the care partner, during this time too. In the providence of God, you have been enrolled, perhaps reluctantly, in God's school of character development. In this school, the entire curriculum is designed to achieve one main goal: Christlikeness. This curriculum often becomes more difficult for caregivers as time goes on, but this is because God is preparing His students for great things.

The development of Christlike character can only take place in the laboratory of real-life experiences known as "adversity." No one wants to go through hard times, but as you may already have discovered, challenges are part of the caregiving journey. If you are wishing you could drop out of school, consider two things. First, you did not enroll yourself in God's "caregiver school"; God Himself enrolled you. He chooses His students and He alone knows how best to teach them. Second, throughout history, God has prepared people to fulfill His call on their lives by first sending them to His school. In the Bible, the lives of Joseph, Jacob, Moses, Ruth, Job, Paul, Peter, and others testify to this. In the modern era, D. L. Moody, Charles Colson, Fanny Crosby, Hudson Taylor, Beth Moore, and countless others experienced some humbling or painful adversity before they could fully embrace God's great purpose for their lives.

God's ways are not our ways. That's why He asks us to walk by faith, not by sight, human wisdom, or human logic. His will for us is often counterintuitive (contrary to what we reason or expect), and we sometimes learn more of God in the shadows than when our path is brightly lit. Charles Haddon Spurgeon, "the prince of preachers," put it this way: "When my schoolroom is darkened, I see the most."

Is your caregiver schoolroom darker than you would like? Even secular wisdom acknowledges that "when the student is ready, the teacher will appear." Be attentive. Your most important lessons may be about to begin!

When my schoolroom is darkened, I see the most.
—CHARLES HADDON SPURGEON

REFLECTIONS ON *CAREGIVER SCHOOL*

If you did not aspire or choose to become a dementia caregiver, how do you feel about being enrolled in "God's school of character development"?

"When my schoolroom is darkened, I see the most." Do you think this statement by Charles Spurgeon is true? Why or why not?

My journal . . .

Why?

*Trust in the Lord with all your
heart, and do not lean on your own understanding.*

PROVERBS 3:5 (ESV)

It had been a surprising new beginning for Mary Ellen.
After surviving the heartbreak of divorce in her for-
ties, she had resigned herself to the fact that she would
live the rest of her life as a single woman. In her wildest
dreams, she never expected to find love again. But a few
years later, she met Dave. They began dating, and in just
a few short months, Mary Ellen knew that she had been
given the wonderful gift of a second chance at love.

She and Dave had been happily married for only three
years when Dave was diagnosed with early-onset Alzheimer's disease. Bitterly disappointed, Mary Ellen began
to slowly let go of her dreams about how she and Dave
would spend the rest of their lives together. She didn't
hesitate to pour out her anger and confusion to God.
"Why, Lord?" she stormed. "Why would you bring Dave
into my life and then let this awful disease spoil our fu-

ture? Why would You do this to me? I don't understand!"

Do you share Mary Ellen's confusion and anger? Is "Why, Lord?" your most impassioned prayer? No matter how heartfelt or sincere, your *why* questions may remain unanswered on this side of heaven. This presents a challenge: can you believe that God is worthy of your trust even when the *why* eludes you?

Whenever we do not understand God's purposes or methods, we are challenged to deepen our confidence in the character and heart of God.

Whate'er It Be

> I take my portion from Thy hand,
> And do not seek to understand;
> For I am blind, while Thou dost see,
> Thy will is mine, whate'er it be.
>
> Thus calmly do I face my lot,
> Accept it, Lord, and doubt Thee not;
> Lo! All things work for good to me;
> Thy will is mine, whate'er it be.[1]

Can you believe that God is worthy of your trust even when the why eludes you?

REFLECTIONS ON *WHY*

What is your response to the song lyrics below?

Thus calmly do I face my lot,
Accept it, Lord, and doubt Thee not;
Lo! All things work for good to me;
Thy will is mine, whate'er it be.

Have you been able to "doubt Thee not" despite your
unanswered *why* questions? If not, speak or write a
prayer below expressing your struggle to release your
unanswered questions to Him.

My journal . . .

Stay Where You Are

*I am the vine; you are the branches. Whoever abides
in me and I in him, he it is that bears much fruit,
for apart from me you can do nothing.*

JOHN 15:5 (ESV)

Andrew, a man with a debilitating chronic illness, said that since he has become housebound due to his disease, "God has felt more absent than perhaps any other time in my life." During this most difficult time of his life, he says, God has seemed the most silent.

Perhaps you can relate. As a caregiver, especially if you are housebound along with the person who has dementia, you too may feel distant from God or feel that He has gone silent. Some of the Old Testament writers felt this way. Psalmists David and Asaph implored God not to be silent:

"God of my praise, do not be silent."—David, Psalm 109:1 (CSB)

"God, do not keep silent. Do not be deaf, God; do not be quiet."—Asaph, Psalm 83:1 (CSB)

Isaiah observed, "Truly, you are a God who hides himself, O God of Israel, the Savior."—Isaiah 45:15 (ESV)

Today we have an advantage that David, Asaph, and Isaiah did not have: God dwells within us in the person of the Holy Spirit. What's more, we know that God is both immutable (incapable of change) and omnipresent (perpetually present everywhere at once). So, since God lives within us, and has not moved and does not change, why do we still sometimes feel distant from Him?

You've probably heard someone say, "If you don't feel close to God, guess who moved?" At first, this modern-day proverb seems to ring true: if God hasn't moved, then any lack of closeness can only be the fault of the person, right? But what if you haven't moved? What if you are earnestly seeking God, reading His Word and praying every day, and you still don't feel close to Him? Maybe blogger Addie Zierman has it exactly right. She wrote,

> *If you feel far away from God, maybe it's possible that no one moved. Not God, of course. But maybe not you either. Maybe this is just a normal part of the long work of faith. Maybe the silence of God is not a*

*punishment but an invitation to a new kind of trust
. . . We've forgotten that God has a habit of going
quiet with his people. If you don't feel God right now,
if you don't hear him and you desperately want to,
be still. It's possible that you're exactly where you're
supposed to be. Rest in the quiet certainty of your own
Belovedness. Stay where you are.*[1]

Jesus gave us a word that means "stay where you are."
The word is *abide*. It's the verb form of *abode*, which means
"dwelling place." Jesus, who dwells in us, invites us to also
dwell in Him: "Abide in me, and I in you . . . As the Father
has loved me, so have I loved you. Abide in my love."[2, 3]

Don't worry about *feeling* close to God; feelings come
and go. Just abide.

> *Maybe the silence of God is an invitation
> to a new kind of trust.*

REFLECTIONS ON *STAY WHERE YOU ARE*

What do you think about Addie Zierman's blog post?

How can you abide in Jesus even when you do not feel emotionally close to Him?

My journal . . .

Day 6

Jars of Clay

Dear friend, I hope all is well with you and that you are as healthy in body as you are strong in spirit.

3 JOHN 1:2

Caring for a person with dementia can be stressful. When stress is unrelenting, it can take a serious toll on the care partner's health. Max, Connie, Camille, and Sam all know this firsthand. Max said, "There is no question that the stress of this disease has been problematic. My health is horrible." Newly diagnosed with type-2 diabetes, Connie admits, "Because I worry and take care of my husband, I forget myself. It has taken a physical toll on me."

Camille said, "I have always been a walker, and now I am too depressed to walk. Walking would help my depression, but at the end of the day, I am just spent." After Sam's wife, Alison, became less mobile due to her Alzheimer's disease, he spent a lot of time "just sitting with her and loving on her, but not doing a lot of physical activity." As a result, he admits, "I was getting to be a tubby fellow."

Health problems, depression, and weight gain or loss are common among stressed-out dementia caregivers. Fortunately, Max, Connie, Camille, and Sam all wisely recognized the need to take better care of themselves, seeking both medical care and counseling. Sam decided he "had to start exercising" and he successfully brought his weight under control. All four also joined a caregiver support group.

Paul described Christians as "jars of clay" that house the precious, eternal treasures of God. Because human "clay" is mortal and fragile, it can be irreparably damaged by the stress and exhaustion of caregiving. Wise caregivers realize that in order to provide good care for their loved one, they *must* take care of their own physical, emotional, and spiritual needs. Caring for your own body, mind, and soul isn't selfish. Rather, it is a vital stewardship entrusted to you by the God who loves you. Is there an aspect of your self-care that you have neglected?

Caring for your own body, mind, and soul isn't selfish. Rather, it is a vital stewardship entrusted to you by the God who loves you.

REFLECTIONS ON *JARS OF CLAY*

Using a scale of 1–5 stars, circle the number of stars that reflects how well you are doing in each aspect of self-care below (1 star = poor; 5 stars = excellent).

emotional   ★ ★ ★ ★ ★
spiritual   ★ ★ ★ ★ ★
physical   ★ ★ ★ ★ ★
social   ★ ★ ★ ★ ★

If there are aspects of your self-care that you have neglected, prayerfully brainstorm here some ways to address these.

My journal . . .

Irritations

*For when the way is rough, your patience has
a chance to grow. So let it grow, and don't try to squirm
out of your problems. For when your patience is finally in full
bloom, then you will be ready for anything, strong in
character, full and complete.*

JAMES 1:3–4 (TLB)

April is the primary care partner for her husband,
Sean, who has early-onset Alzheimer's disease. As
a loving wife, April tries hard to respond patiently to
the irritations that come about due to Sean's cognitive
decline.

"There's no point in trying to reason with him," April
explained. "There's no point in saying, 'Do you realize
how irritating that is?'" April knows that Sean is not intentionally trying to annoy her. She also realizes that irritations are bound to occur when living with a person who
has dementia. Yet April also acknowledges that, from an
emotional standpoint, irritations are so . . . irritating!

If oysters could talk, they would surely empathize

with care partners like April. Oysters know a thing or two about irritations.

Occasionally, a foreign substance, usually a parasite or a shell particle, works its way into an oyster's shell. Once inside, it gets stuck in the creature's soft inner body. This intruder irritates the oyster's body wall, the mantle. The mantle responds to the irritation by secreting a substance called nacre (NAY-ker). Nacre is a smooth, hard crystalline substance, also known as mother-of-pearl. For as long as the irritant remains within the shell, the mantle will continue to dispense the silky nacre. Over time, as layer after layer of nacre surrounds and coats the irritant, a lustrous pearl is formed. Unlike gemstones that need to be cut and polished to reveal their beauty, pearls are already naturally lustrous and lovely when they are harvested.

Pearls are a natural metaphor for a spiritual truth. Just as an oyster turns its irritants into valuable, beautiful pearls, God can turn our irritations into a pearl of a different sort: character qualities that mirror Jesus. As we surrender to God the situations and circumstances that provoke us, our patience grows and our Christlikeness increases, transforming our irritations into pearls.

Pearls are a natural metaphor for a spiritual truth.

REFLECTIONS ON *IRRITATIONS*

Are you willing to allow God to turn the irritations of caregiving into "pearls" of Christlike character?

If so, how can you invite the Lord into the situations that irritate you?

My journal . . .

_____

_____

_____

_____

He Knew

Your eyes saw my unformed body; all the days ordained for me were written in your book before one of them came to be.

PSALM 139:16 (NIV)

I laughed along with the rest of the class when our Bible teacher told us, "There has never been a time when God has said, 'Wow, I never saw *that* coming!'" We laughed because we understood the impossibility of such a moment: God alone is all knowing (omniscient). Nothing has ever escaped His notice; nothing ever will. God alone "sees it coming"—down to the smallest detail. Nothing ever catches Him by surprise.

Unlike God, we cannot see what lies ahead. As the years of our lives unfold, we encounter one surprise after another. Sometimes the surprises are pleasant: a phone call from an old friend who is back in town or the first glimpse of snowflakes falling on Christmas morning. Other times, the surprises are extraordinarily painful, stabbing at our hearts and making us cry. Though perplexing and inexplicable from our human perspective, God writes both kinds of surprises into the story of every life.

A loved one's diagnosis of Alzheimer's disease or another dementia is always the unwelcome, heartrending kind of surprise. No one ever sees it coming. The news is always a shock, not only for the person with the disease, but also for the loved ones unwittingly thrust into a role they never planned to fill: caregiver.

Allow yourself to marvel at this, caregiving child of God: your heavenly Father has always known this time in your life would arrive. Before you were even born, He foresaw your days as a caregiver. You are part of His plan for your loved one; your loved one is part of His plan for you. Take His hand and let Him quell your fears as you walk each new day on the shepherding path before you.

You are part of God's plan for your loved one;
your loved one is part of God's plan for you.

REFLECTIONS ON *HE KNEW*

What do you think and feel when you ponder Psalm 139:16?

Do you believe that the relationship between you and the person for whom you provide care is part of God's plan for both of your lives? Explain why you do or do not believe this.

My journal . . .

Cherish What Remains

Therefore, as we have opportunity, let us do good to all people, especially to those who belong to the family of believers.

GALATIANS 6:10 (NIV)

Human relationships are like tapestries. As the years go by, all the "fibers" of life—shared experiences, conversations, good times and bad times—intertwine to weave a unique and beautiful marriage, family, or friendship. When Alzheimer's disease or another kind of dementia enters the picture, it causes the tapestry to slowly unravel. The design that was so lovingly woven becomes distorted as the disease relentlessly pulls at the fibers that once entwined to create it.

Dementia unravels relational tapestries from both sides. When dementia is diagnosed, healthy family members may take a step back from the person with the disease, either intentionally or unintentionally, to get their bearings. What does this terrible diagnosis mean? They may be fearful: How will dementia change this loved one? How will it alter their emotional connection with this person? There may be grief as they realize that some of their dreams and goals for the future may now be lost. And if they belong to a social or ethnic community that attaches any stigma to dementia, they may be coping with embarrassment or shame as well.

At the same time, the newly diagnosed person may also be stepping back from the relationship. If they are early in their disease, they too may be dealing with fear, grief, and feeling stigmatized. If their disease is further along, they may be stepping back from loved ones due to the disease itself. Personality changes, decreased ability to take initiative, and waning interest in social connection may all occur with the progression of the disease.

For both people, the greatest sadness may be the fact that dementia will one day fully unravel the tapestry of their relationship. This realization can inspire within caregivers a great resolve to celebrate each day of the dementia journey that remains. To accomplish this, a change in mindset may be needed: at every stage of the disease, there is now a need to focus not on what has been lost, but on what remains.

As your loved one's care partner, remember that as their disease progresses, the most important questions to consider at each stage will always be:

- What can the person with dementia still do without assistance?

- What does he or she still enjoy or take pleasure in?

- What activities can he or she still share in with family and friends?

The answers to these questions will guide you and your family in making the most of the time that remains with your loved one. Resolve, with God's help, to make the remainder of your loved one's dementia journey as beautiful, meaningful, and full of love as possible.

Resolve to celebrate each day that remains in your loved one's dementia journey.

REFLECTIONS ON *CHERISH WHAT REMAINS*

How well are you dealing with any fear, grief, or sense of stigma you may still feel related to your loved one's dementia diagnosis?

What might help you resolve these feelings?

How has your loved one's dementia begun to unravel the "tapestry" of your relationship?

My journal . . .

Day 10

Caregiver Anger

Human anger does not produce the righteousness God desires.
JAMES 1:20

I am experiencing anger," one caregiver said. "And while I know it stems from hurt, the anguish of long-term caretaking, I don't know where to turn. My parents are manipulative, ungrateful, and downright dishonest. There is *no* appreciation for what I do, and it is very difficult for me to carve out time for myself, so I have found myself getting resentful."[1]

It is not hard to understand this daughter's anger. Anger is a normal human emotion that emerges when we feel we have been deliberately wronged in some way. Caregivers may experience anger if they:

- Feel they had no choice about becoming a caregiver
- Don't have enough help and support
- Feel unappreciated or taken for granted
- Are exhausted, hungry, or lonely

Anger in and of itself is neither good nor bad; it's just a powerful emotion. Its "goodness" or "badness" depends on how it is expressed. Anger can be a good thing when it propels us to right a wrong or seek a solution. Anger becomes a bad thing when it festers to the point of bitterness or spins out of control, resulting in harmful or sinful behavior toward others or even toward the person with dementia.

So how does God want exasperated caregivers to handle their anger? While it's understandable to feel angry about injustice and ungodly behavior, the apostle Paul cautioned, "In your anger do not sin: Do not let the sun go down while you are still angry" (Ephesians 4:26 NIV).

Based on Paul's counsel, here are two suggestions:

- First, resolve to discharge the energy produced by anger in a nondestructive way such as exercising, journaling, hammering a nail, punching a pillow, or cleaning the house.

- Second, recognize that some anger-provoking things can be changed, while others are beyond our control. Once you determine which is the case, ask God for wisdom and guidance about how to respond in your personal situation as you meditate on what the Bible says about anger.

Anger in and of itself is neither good nor bad;
it's just a powerful emotion.

REFLECTIONS ON *CAREGIVER ANGER*

If you are experiencing anger, consider meditating on some of the verses below over the next several days. Note the ideas that particularly stand out to you. Let these verses guide you in addressing this area of your life.

WISDOM: Proverbs 12:16; Proverbs 14:29; Proverbs 19:11; Proverbs 22:24–25

GUIDANCE: James 1:19–20; Ephesians 4:31; Colossians 3:8; Matthew 5:21–22; Jonah 4

JESUS' ANGER: Matthew 21:12–13; Mark 3:4–6; Mark 10:13–14

GOD'S ANGER: Exodus 34:6; Psalm 30:5; Psalm 78:38; Psalm 103:8–9; 1 Thessalonians 5:9

My journal . . .

What About Me?

We know that God has chosen you, dear brothers,
much beloved of God.

1 THESSALONIANS 1:4 (TLB)

Carla, Harry, and Bruce are all full-time caregivers for their spouses with dementia. The three are members of the same caregiver support group. Bruce told the group that his wife is now growing unsteady on her feet. She recently fell when the couple was away from home. Bruce is finding that in order to provide more vigilant care and supervision for his wife, he must now often set his own wishes aside. He lamented, "Whatever *I* want isn't in the picture."

Carla understands. She said, "It is really like taking care of a child, a child who is perpetually sick and you don't get any significant breaks."

Harry observed, "There are so many ironies. One of them is that at the very time when the caregiver needs to be the one who does everything, the person in their care needs more time and more touch and more of the things that keep you from getting the tasks of life done."

The constant, selfless service that these caregivers willingly provide leaves no doubt that they dearly love their spouses. When caregivers continually devote most of their time, energy, and attention to a person with dementia, however, it's easy to lose perspective. Because they are so intently focused on the constant needs of their loved one, caregivers may devalue or even ignore their own physical, emotional, and spiritual needs in order to stay focused on the person with dementia. When a loved one's needs continually overshadow the caregiver's needs, it can slowly erode the caregiver's sense of worth and cloud their perception of God's love.

If your caregiving experience is sometimes difficult or unpleasant, and if your personal needs often go unmet, do you sometimes think, "Hey, what about me?" Do you wonder, "Does God even care about what I am going through?" The answer, of course, is yes, God does care about you and about what you are going through. He cares even when (maybe *especially* when) the stress and exhaustion of caregiving has skewed your perception of His concern for you.

We humans have things in proper perspective only when we see ourselves as God sees us. When you are stressed out or exhausted from caregiving, how does God see you? When your needs are "on hold" because the needs of the person with dementia are more urgent, how does God see you? He sees you—always—through the eyes of His compassion. He sees you—always—as who you really are: His own precious, beloved child for whom He cares more deeply than you can imagine. Even when you are too worn out to *feel* this truth, let it resonate in your heart: "See how very much our heavenly Father loves us, for he allows us to be called his children—think of it—and we really *are*!" (1 John 3:1a TLB). This is who God is, and this is who you are, and nothing you will ever experience as a caregiver can ever alter that.

Do you sometimes wonder, "Does God even care about what I'm going through?"

REFLECTIONS ON *WHAT ABOUT ME?*

In 1 Thessalonians 1:4, what do the words "much beloved of God" and "chosen" tell you about your value to God?

When you are stressed out or exhausted from caregiving or when your needs are "on hold" because the needs of the person with dementia are more urgent, how do you view *yourself*?

Do your feelings and your view of yourself make it easier or more difficult to believe God loves and cares for you?

My journal . . .

The Power of Music

Praise the LORD, for the LORD is good;
celebrate his lovely name with music.

PSALM 135:3

Music can touch the emotions of a person with Alzheimer's disease as nothing else can. Sometimes it evokes such surprising depth of feeling that only a word like "magical" can describe it. My friend Karolyn (whose husband, Gary, wrote the foreword to this book) has witnessed this personally.

Karolyn and her brother Bobby had gone to visit another brother, Gene, in a long-term care facility. Once a brilliant university professor, Gene was now in the final stage of Alzheimer's disease. His demeanor was stoic and he was unresponsive to his visitors. He did not speak, make eye contact, or respond to their touch. Nevertheless, Karolyn and Bobby decided to sing to him.

Experts say that "reminiscence music," the songs that were popular during a person's teens and twenties, are most likely to impact those with advanced dementia.

Knowing this, Karolyn deliberately chose songs from Gene's early years. Hoping to see a reaction, she and Bobby sang "You Are My Sunshine." Gene was unresponsive. Next, still hopeful, they sang "Somewhere Over the Rainbow." Again, there was no response. Undaunted, they tried once more. This time, as the strains of "Jesus Loves Me" filled the air, Karolyn and Bobby were astonished and elated to see their brother "come alive." Gene's eyes filled with tears. He turned his body toward them and reached out his hand to touch them!

One month after this amazing and memorable moment, Gene passed away.

Because music can have such a dramatic impact, many dementia care partners use music to help manage the behaviors and daily routine of the person in their care. Music can help improve mood and behavior, reduce aggression and agitation, and lower anxiety. For both patient and care partner, music lowers cortisol, the "fight-or-flight" hormone generated by stress.

Music is mentioned throughout the Bible. In Zephaniah, God sings over His people as an expression of His great love for them:

> *The LORD your God is in your midst, a mighty one who will save; he will rejoice over you with gladness; he will quiet you by his love; he will exult over you with loud singing.*[1]

In the Psalms, God's people worship Him through music:

> Praise the LORD, for the LORD is good; celebrate his lovely name with music.[2]

The book of Revelation tells us that all of history will culminate with singing:

> And then I heard every creature in heaven and on earth and under the earth and in the sea. They sang: "Blessing and honor and glory and power belong to the one sitting on the throne and to the Lamb forever and ever."[3]

Clearly, music enables humanity to magnify and praise God as He deserves. Thus, music blesses both God and people. In the context of Alzheimer's disease, as we have seen, music has extra-special importance.

You can use music to help create a warm and calming environment that benefits both you and the person with dementia. Worshipful music can help you maintain a positive focus throughout the day. Observe the effect of your music choices on the person in your care—if a song brings joy, keep it on your playlist. If he or she grew up attending church, Christian music may trigger deep emotion, as it did for Gene. It may even be that God can use Christian music to supernaturally draw those with dementia to Himself despite their cognitive deficits.

Worshipful music can calm and comfort both care partners and those with dementia.

REFLECTIONS ON *THE POWER OF MUSIC*

What effect does worshipful music have on your thoughts and mood?

What effect do you think an atmosphere of Christian music in your home might have on your caregiving? On the person for whom you provide care?

My journal . . . .

Day 13

Feeling Guilty

For your faithful love guides me, and I live by your truth.

PSALM 26:3 (CSB)

Jake's wife has Alzheimer's disease. He said, "You want to do everything you can to make it as good for them as possible. Then you get that guilt: *you're never going to make it as good as you want it to be.* I feel like I could do so much for her. I just keep dropping the ball. It's because I can't fix it. I can't make her better. What do you call it—survivor guilt?"

Megan, whose mother provides care for her dad, already feels guilty about what would happen if the caregiving should fall to her. She said, "I know that I could not physically take care of my dad if he had to live with us." But when she thinks about placing him in a facility, she feels guilty: "I don't like feeling that I am just discarding him."

Art understands how Megan feels. He believes it is his duty to care for his wife at home. He said, "I'd be so ridden with guilt if I moved her into a facility I don't know if I could live with myself."[1]

Jake, Megan, and Art are typical of many family caregivers. No matter how much they do for their loved one, they feel guilty about not doing more. Many also feel guilty when they take time for themselves. Some feel guilty simply because they are cognitively normal and their loved one is not. Still others feel guilty for placing their loved one in a facility even when they know it was the very best decision.

It is important to recognize the difference between true guilt and false guilt. True guilt is from God; it is an indicator that your conscience is working! When we have wronged someone, the Holy Spirit makes us aware of our sin and our sense of guilt leads us to confess our sin to God and to the person we have offended. False guilt is another matter.

One writer said, "So many of us suffer with false guilt; we take moral responsibility for actions, events, and situations that were not our fault. False guilt has no value; it is always detrimental. Where does false guilt come from? False accusations can come from other people . . . from our own self-talk (if I hadn't insisted on going out to dinner, we wouldn't have had the accident). Satan is the primary source of false guilt. He is called the nefarious 'accuser of the brothers' (Revelation 12:10)."[2]

When feelings of guilt are not the result of wrongdoing, when there is no one with whom you need to make amends, caregiver guilt can be reframed as whatever it really is. It may be the point at which your desire to do more for your loved one collides with the reality that you cannot. It may be regret over not making the most of the time you had with your loved one before dementia. It may be sadness about how the disease is affecting your loved one, your family, and you.

Are you weighed down with guilt for things that are not your fault? Do you feel guilty for things that are not morally wrong? Reframing your guilt feelings in the truth, whatever it may be, will set you free from the burden of false guilt.

Reframing your guilt feelings in truth will set you free from the burden of false guilt.

REFLECTIONS ON *FEELING GUILTY*

What dementia-related or caregiving-related issues do you feel guilty about? List them here.

Circle anything on your list that is not your fault and/or is not morally wrong. Ask God to help you think differently about these sources of false guilt.

If there are items on your list that are creating true guilt, confess them to God and accept His forgiveness. If you need to also make amends with anyone, ask God to guide you in taking that step.

My journal . . .

Gratitude

Therefore let us be grateful for receiving a kingdom that cannot be shaken, and thus let us offer to God acceptable worship, with reverence and awe . . .

HEBREWS 12:28 (ESV)

In recent years, researchers have become interested in the effects of gratitude. They have discovered that an attitude of gratitude is surprisingly powerful. In one study, people wrote in a journal once a week, writing just five sentences: one sentence each about five things for which they felt grateful. In just two months, there were "significant" effects. Compared to a group that did not write about gratitude, the journal keepers were happier, more optimistic, and reported fewer physical problems. They even worked out more often than the comparison group.[1]

Mental health experts link the habit of counting one's blessings—gratitude —to resilience. In fact, some say that gratitude is the *key* to resilience. The American Psychological Association defines *resilience* as "the process of adapting well in the face of adversity, trauma, tragedy, threats or significant sources of stress."[2] The Merriam-Webster dictionary offers an even simpler definition: "the ability to become strong, healthy, or successful again after something bad happens."

If you are a husband, wife, or adult child who has been unexpectedly thrust into a caregiving role by a loved one's dementia, you may indeed feel that "something bad" has happened to your family. You may feel that the responsibilities of caregiving have added "adversity, trauma . . . or significant sources of stress" to your life. As a Christ-follower, you are no doubt endeavoring to process your feelings and respond to your circumstances in the context of your faith. Even so, gratitude may seem foreign (or even inappropriate) to you right now. Yet cultivating a heartfelt sense of gratitude may be the single most important step you can take toward developing the resilience you need for the caregiving journey.

Gratitude isn't an all-or-nothing proposition. It's specific. For a moment, let your thoughts drift across the people in your life. Think about friends, family members, coworkers, the people at your church, and the Lord Himself. Think about music, pets, your work, medical care, food, clothing, shelter, and all else that touches your life. What thoughts spark feelings of gratitude? As you meditate on these blessings, plant the gratitude you feel deep in your heart. A grateful heart will help you bounce back on bad days—that's resilience!

A grateful heart will help you bounce back on bad days.

REFLECTIONS ON *GRATITUDE*

Identify five things for which you are grateful and write one sentence about each of them.

List your biggest disappointments and identify one aspect of each for which you can choose to be grateful.

My journal . . .

I AM

Then Moses asked God, "If I go to the Israelites and say to
them, 'The God of your fathers has sent me to you,' and they
ask me, 'What is his name?' what should I tell them?"
God replied to Moses, "I AM WHO I AM. This is what you
are to say to the Israelites: I AM has sent me to you."

EXODUS 3:13–14 (CSB)

Although God has always existed, His name is not I WAS. Though He will continue to exist forever, His name is not I WILL BE. Our God is I AM, the God of the eternal present. As the Creator of time, He can operate outside of time. To God, every day of the past and every day of the future are the same as the present moment in which you are reading these words.

The Jews of Jesus' day all recognized I AM as the name of God. The religious establishment became furious when Jesus rightfully claimed this name as proof of His deity as God the Son:

> *"You are not yet fifty years old," they said to him,*
> *"and you have seen Abraham!"*
>
> *"Very truly I tell you," Jesus answered, "before*
> *Abraham was born, I am!" At this, they picked up*
> *stones to stone him, but Jesus hid himself, slipping*
> *away from the temple grounds.* (John 8:57–59 NIV)

After His resurrection, Jesus underscored for His disciples (including all of us) the meaning of I AM. When He said, "I am with you always, even to the end of the world" (Matthew 28:20 TLB), Jesus was again identifying Himself as I AM, the God of the eternal present. There is incredible comfort for caregivers not only in Christ's identity as I AM, but also in what this qualifies Him alone to promise: He is with us all day every day and He will never leave us. As the God of the eternal present, there is no moment of your day that is not fully in the view of I AM. He is present with you perpetually, 24/7.

Through the ages, God has continually assured His people, "I AM here." This is His assurance to you, personally, as well. You can confidently lean upon the psalmist's assertion that "God is our refuge and strength, a *very present* help in trouble" (Psalm 46:1 ESV). Assurances such as this about the constant presence of God are found throughout the Bible. Maggie, whose husband has Alzheimer's, intentionally relies upon these assurances. She depends on God's "very present" daily help for all the ups and downs of her sometimes stressful, sometimes sorrowful caregiving journey. She said, "I turn to God's Word every day because it gives me the strength as a caregiver to know that I'm not alone, that God is there and He's helping me." Her statement "I'm not alone . . . God is there" reveals that she truly believes God's promise: *I AM here.*

There is no moment of your day that is not fully in the view of I AM.

REFLECTIONS ON *I AM*

How can an awareness of God's constant presence help you as you care for your loved one?

Maggie has made a habit of reading God's Word every day. Through this daily connection with *I AM*, she continually receives comfort and strength for her caregiving journey. Do you experience God as Maggie does, as your personal daily "refuge and strength"? If not, consider making it your practice to connect with God daily through His Word. If your present schedule makes this difficult, what changes could you make to ensure time for meeting with God each day?

My journal . . .

Day 16

Ask!

Two are better than one, because they have a good reward for their toil. For if they fall, one will lift up his fellow. But woe to him who is alone when he falls and has not another to lift him up!

ECCLESIASTES 4:9–10 (ESV)

When we trip and fall, it's much easier to get back on our feet if someone is there to help us. As the writer of Ecclesiastes observed, however, it's "woe" if we fall when there is no one around to help. For the dementia caregiver, falls are not usually the kind caused by gravity. The isolation, exhaustion, and stress of caregiving can make one more vulnerable to "falls" that are emotional, spiritual, or moral.

Have you been thinking of caregiving as a solo endeavor—something that is your sole responsibility? If so, it's time to change your paradigm. Going forward, think of caregiving as a "team sport." Every caregiver needs a team of people to help carry the load. Those who don't have a team are more likely to burn out or bail out. Carol, who has been on the dementia journey with her husband for five years, said that caregiving is "the most difficult thing I've ever done in my sixty-something years on this earth." She admits, "I have tried to play a team sport by myself. And I feel like my health is suffering because of this." Sarah, who has been her husband's care partner for six years, said she has come to the realization that "it's impossible to do it alone."

Solo caregiving is like trying to carry a sofa down a flight of stairs by yourself. For some things, we've just got to have the help of others to shoulder the load. When you reach the point in your caregiving journey where you need help, it's time to ask!

Start by asking God for wisdom—who might be able to help? Make a list of potential care team members: friends, those in your faith community, extended family members, neighbors, and others. Then simply share with them what stage the disease is in, and the specific kinds of help you need.

Not everyone will be able or willing to join your team, but you may be surprised to find many people who have always been willing to help, but just didn't know how—until you asked!

Solo caregiving is like trying to carry a sofa down a flight of stairs by yourself.

REFLECTIONS ON *ASK!*

Is it difficult for you to ask others for help? If so, why do you think this is true?

Prayerfully brainstorm below a list of people you might ask to join your "caregiver team." Beside each name, jot a way that person might be able to assist you.

My journal . . .

Everything to God in Prayer

... pray without ceasing ...

1 THESSALONIANS 5:17 (ESV)

In 1845, a twenty-five-year-old Irish man, Joseph Scriven, stood on the bank of the River Bann, watching as his fiancée crossed a bridge on horseback, making her way toward him. Tragically, before she could reach the place where Joseph stood, she fell from her horse and drowned. It was the day before their wedding.

Not long after, the grief-stricken young man made the long voyage across the Atlantic to Canada. Starting over in this new country, Joseph worked as a tutor and a lay preacher. Years later, at age thirty-nine, he fell in love again. The bride-to-be was the lovely Miss Eliza Catherine Roche, just twenty-two years old. Unbelievably, before they could marry, Eliza died of pneumonia.

Joseph Scriven never married. He devoted the rest of his life to tutoring, preaching, and performing acts of Christian charity. After his death in 1886, the city of Port Hope, Ontario, Canada, erected a monument to his life.

Scriven is best known for a poem he wrote in 1855 to comfort his mother, who was seriously ill in Ireland. Perhaps drawing deeply from his own journey through grief, he titled the poem *Pray Without Ceasing*.

Today we know his words as the lyrics of the beloved hymn, *What a Friend We Have in Jesus.* The words are as comforting and encouraging to dementia care partners today as they surely must have been to Scriven's mother more than a century and a half ago:[1, 2, 3]

What a Friend We Have in Jesus

What a friend we have in Jesus,
All our sins and griefs to bear!
What a privilege to carry
Everything to God in prayer!
Oh, what peace we often forfeit,
Oh, what needless pain we bear,
All because we do not carry
Everything to God in prayer!

What a friend we have in Jesus!

REFLECTIONS ON
EVERYTHING TO GOD IN PRAYER

Which words or phrases in Joseph Scriven's poem stand out to you? Why are they meaningful?

What does "pray without ceasing" mean to you?

My journal . . .

Day 18

Bad Day

Weeping may last through the night,
but joy comes with the morning.

PSALM 30:5B

Has your computer ever just seemed to "hang"? You've clicked or double-clicked, expecting a certain response, but nothing happens. All progress is suspended, and you wait and wait, but nothing changes. Finally, with a sigh, you shut it all down, then start it all back up again. This reboot gets everything moving again as it should.

Very likely, you have had some days when things "hang" just like that. Nothing goes as you had hoped. Things go from bad to worse as the day goes on. By late afternoon you are exhausted and the person in your care continues to try your patience on into the evening. Your ability to cope grows thinner by the hour. Finally, you heave a sigh and decide to give up for the day. The only thing left to do is reboot. After all, as the saying goes, tomorrow is another day.

Jesus knew we would all have "bad" days—ones that include more struggles and disappointments than we know how to handle. We should not really be surprised; troublesome days are part of living in this fallen, imperfect world. Jesus acknowledged this when He said, "In this world you will have trouble"[1] and "Each day has enough trouble of its own."[2]

Along with His affirmation that, yes, some days will be like that, He also reminded us that all of this is temporary. The fuller context of the verses above gives us the eternal perspective:

> *I have told you these things, so that in me you may have peace. In this world you will have trouble. But take heart! I have overcome the world.*[1]
>
> *Therefore don't worry about tomorrow, because tomorrow will worry about itself. Each day has enough trouble of its own.*[2]

God has told us that trouble is to be expected. In His mercy, He has also provided for us the way to reboot after a bad day. The reboot comes as we release our bad day to Him, recharge our bodies and minds with sleep, and awake to start over in a brand-new day. He Himself is the best part of our reboot; He meets us each morning in a fresh, new way:

"The faithful love of the LORD never ends! His mercies never cease. Great is his faithfulness; his mercies begin afresh each morning."[3]

After a bad day, reboot!

REFLECTIONS ON *BAD DAY*

What do the words "his mercies begin afresh each morning" (Lamentations 3:22–23) mean to you?

How difficult is it for you to "reboot" (release your bad day to God, recharge yourself with sleep, and awaken to start over in a new day)?

Which of the three steps is most difficult for you? Which is easiest? Why?

My journal . . .

_____

_____

_____

_____

_____

_____

_____

_____

_____

_____

Day 19

Surrogate Family

Plans go wrong for lack of advice;
many advisers bring success.

PROVERBS 15:22

When Sonja was struggling to deal with her husband's dementia, she reached out to her siblings for support. To Sonja's great disappointment, they were unsupportive. One sister told her, "I have an issue with you talking about how hard this is for you when your husband is the one who is losing his life." Realizing that her family would not be there for her, Sonja turned to her "surrogate family," the members of her church—and they *did* come through.

The diagnosis of dementia is difficult news for any couple or family to process. When relationships have been loving and close for many years, family members are well prepared to circle around the person with dementia and to work together as a caregiving team. When a family has a history of discord prior to dementia, coping with dementia can be more challenging and complicated. If divorce and/or remarriage have occurred, or when a couple was already emotionally distant before one spouse developed dementia, the caregiving spouse may need extra support to successfully weather the years ahead. Without strong social support, dementia can stress relationships to the breaking point.

While every caregiver needs practical help and social support, this support is even more vital for those whose family members are unsupportive or estranged. As Sonja learned, support can come from sources other than one's biological family. Friends, one's faith community, neighbors, coworkers, and a dementia support group are all potential components of your "surrogate family." Counseling from professionals who understand dementia and dementia caregiving can also be especially valuable to those like Sonja whose family circumstances are difficult. This kind of "talk therapy" helps address the emotions, worries, and patient behaviors that arise during the dementia journey. When no professional dementia counseling is locally available, the Alzheimer's Association 24/7 phone helpline counselors may be able to suggest other resources.

No matter what you are facing on your caregiving journey, the Bible encourages you to seek support and wise counsel from multiple sources. It also promises you the help of God Himself:

- Where there is no guidance, a people falls, but in an abundance of counselors there is safety (Proverbs 11:14 ESV).

- The LORD says, "I will guide you along the best pathway for your life. I will advise you and watch over you" (Psalm 32:8).

Social support is especially important for those whose family members are unsupportive or estranged.

REFLECTIONS ON *SURROGATE FAMILY*

Do you feel that you have enough social support and practical help? If not, list some individuals, organizations, and/or helping professionals who might be able to become part of your "surrogate family."

If your answer to the question above was yes, list the people who help and support you and take a moment to thank God for each of them.

My journal . . .

_____

_____

_____

_____

_____

_____

_____

_____

_____

_____

Day 20

Bugs and Oil

You honor me by anointing my head with oil.
My cup overflows with blessings.

PSALM 23:5B

The work of a dementia caregiver is, in many ways, like the work of a good shepherd. Thus, certain insights from the book *A Shepherd Looks at Psalm 23* will resonate deeply with caregivers. The author, W. Phillip Keller, is a former real-life shepherd. Like David the shepherd/psalmist, Keller draws profound spiritual lessons from his shepherding experience. One such lesson comes from the nose fly, a parasite that is particularly bothersome to sheep.

Keller explains, "These little flies buzz about the sheep's head, attempting to deposit their eggs on the damp mucous membranes of the sheep's nose." Once deposited, the eggs hatch and form small, wormlike larvae. These larvae work their way into the sheep's nasal passages and burrow into their flesh, creating inflammation and irritation that sheep find nearly unbearable.

Some sheep, Keller says, "become frantic with fear and panic in their attempt to escape their tormentors." They race around the pasture trying desperately to escape the flies. Some eventually drop from sheer exhaustion; others toss their heads up and down for hours at a time.

With a caring shepherd's compassion, Keller sought to protect his flock from these flies by applying a homemade remedy of linseed oil, sulfur, and tar to their heads and noses. This made an "incredible difference," Keller recalls. "Gone was the aggravation, gone the frenzy, gone the irritability and the restlessness."

Keller goes on to share his personal application of this experience with his flock. He cites first the impact of things that "bug" him (". . . the small, petty annoyances that ruin my repose . . . the niggling distractions that . . . can well-nigh drive me round the bend or up the wall"). Then, he shares the remedy: the gracious, soothing "oil" of the Holy Spirit who "alone makes it possible for us to react to aggravations and annoyances with quietness and calmness."

Keller's "nose fly lesson" is easy to apply to dementia caregiving: there is no shortage of "aggravations and annoyances" when caring for a person with dementia! You may be as "bugged" by odd behaviors, sleep disturbances, forgetfulness, "sundowning" (confusion and agitation that increases later in the day), hallucinations, repeating, wandering, or stubbornness as a sheep plagued by nose flies.

The good news is that the same solution Phillip Keller has identified for himself is fully available to you as well:

> *What I do in any given situation is to expose it to my Master, my Owner, Christ Jesus, and say simply, "O Lord, I can't cope with these petty, annoying, peevish problems. Please apply the oil of Your Spirit to my mind. Both at the conscious and subconscious levels of my thought-life enable me to act and react just as You would." And He will. It will surprise you how promptly He complies with such a request made in deadly earnest.*[1]

Are you "bugged" by the aggravations and annoyances of a person with dementia?

REFLECTIONS ON *BUGS AND OIL*

How are your responses to aggravations and annoyances like those of a sheep afflicted with nose flies?

In what caregiving situations do you most need to apply the gracious, soothing oil of the Holy Spirit?

My journal . . .

Day 21

Caregiver Depression

. . . God, who comforts and encourages the depressed. . .
2 CORINTHIANS 7:6 (AMP)

Seth is the primary caregiver for his wife, Kara, who has frontotemporal dementia (FTD). FTD causes Kara to be rude, emotionally indifferent to her family, and apt to behave in embarrassing, socially inappropriate ways. Seth and Kara's marriage, once close and loving, is now very difficult due to Kara's disease. As a result, Seth battles depression.

Seth is certainly not alone. About 40 percent of family dementia caregivers suffer from depression. In fact, dementia caregivers are twice as likely to become depressed as those who care for people with other conditions. Dementia caregivers are more prone to depression for many reasons, including lack of sleep, coping with stubbornness and behavior problems, having little time for personal pursuits and friends, financial pressures, and lack of help from others. Depression is very complex, however, and is often due to more than the stress of caregiving. Genetic or hormonal factors, having experienced abuse, taking certain medicines, or living with a chronic physical health problem can also make one more prone to depression.

Depression is not the same as feeling sad. Everyone feels "down" or sad from time to time, but these feelings don't last long. True clinical depression is different. It lingers on and on. If you have been feeling hopeless, empty, irritable, and/or fatigued *for two weeks or more*, you may be depressed. Other symptoms can include eating or sleeping too much or too little, tearfulness, feeling numb, easily angered or agitated, or wrestling with thoughts of running away.

If any of this sounds like you, as a Christian your first instinct has likely been to bring your struggles to God in prayer. This is absolutely appropriate! God is tenderly compassionate toward you and fully understands your feelings. As the verse below tells us, God comforts and encourages us in times of depression. God can do this in many ways, but note how He comforted Paul and Timothy: He used a *person*. His name was Titus.

But God, who comforts and encourages the depressed and the disquieted, comforted us by the arrival of Titus.

2 CORINTHIANS 7:6 (AMP)

Before Titus arrived, Paul and Timothy were having a very tough time. The Bible doesn't provide us with a lot of detail, except to say that externally they were facing oppression and affliction on all sides, and internally they were experiencing turmoil, dread, and fear. When Titus showed up with the good news that the Corinthians had responded well to the letter Paul had sent, Paul and Timothy were greatly comforted and cheered.

If you are depressed, God can also use people to comfort and support you. You may be surprised to hear it, but one of the key people God can use is your physician. It's very important to tell your doctor that you are a dementia caregiver and to fully describe how you have been feeling. Since depression is a treatable medical condition, your doctor may prescribe a medication to help lift your mood and improve your sleep, appetite, and concentration. Experts say that the chances for depression increase with the severity of a family member's dementia. With this fact in mind, as your loved one's dementia progresses, pay close attention to your mood and tell your doctor if you recognize symptoms of depression.

If you are depressed, it is also important to talk about your feelings. Many people find that "talk therapy," in combination with antidepressant medication, effectively combats depression. If possible, talk with close friends, trusted family members, and/or your pastor or priest. In addition, seek out a dementia caregiver support group where you can talk openly about your feelings. You can also ask your doctor or pastor to recommend a psychologist, social worker, or licensed therapist who understands the stressful nature of caregiving.

Many people find that daily exercise is another significant help. Exercise triggers the release of endorphins, natural brain chemicals that help reduce depression and anxiety. When prayer, medicine, talk therapy, and exercise are combined, they form a powerful four-pronged weapon against depression!

If you are depressed, it's important to talk about your feelings.

REFLECTIONS ON *CAREGIVER DEPRESSION*

How does your attitude about depression compare with God's (2 Corinthians 7:6)?

With the four-pronged approach to depression in mind, how might God use you to encourage a depressed care-giver?

How can you proactively apply this information to your own life to help prevent depression?

My journal . . .

Day 22

Love Languages

*There are three things that remain—faith, hope, and love—
and the greatest of these is love.*

1 CORINTHIANS 13:13 (TLB)

Everyone needs to feel loved by the significant people in their life. This need for love doesn't disappear with a diagnosis of dementia. According to Dr. Gary Chapman, there are five ways that people express and receive emotional love. With these "love languages," care partners can express love to a person whose memory and cognition are failing.[1]

The love languages used to reach out to those with dementia are:

- PHYSICAL TOUCH: expressive touch such as holding hands or stroking the hair, or instrumental (task-oriented) touch, such as assisting with bathing or dressing

- QUALITY MOMENTS: giving a person with dementia moments of laughter, pleasure, or your undivided attention

- **GIFTS:** purchased, found, or handmade tangible tokens of love or the intangible gift of time

- **WORDS OF AFFIRMATION:** compliments or words of kindness or encouragement

- **ACTS OF KINDNESS:** things done to preserve dignity or make a person feel useful. Examples: including them in a group conversation even if they can't contribute; letting them "help" fold towels

These love languages get through to the person with dementia because, even in the late stages of the disease, people are still emotionally alive. What's more, the feeling of being loved can persist for them even after they forget the actions or words that delivered the love message. Thus, care partners can use the love languages to help create happiness and a good quality of life for the person in their care.

The love languages can meet unspoken emotional needs and ease the frustration of a person with dementia, potentially improving their behavior. With better behavior, the care partner's load is lightened. In cognitively healthy people, one's primary love language doesn't change as the years go by. For those with dementia, the importance of each love language may change as the brain changes. One caregiver observed, "As caregivers, we have to determine what their love language is at each point. It changes. We have to reach out using whatever their love language is right now."

Consider how the combination of three love languages impacted my friend Ingrid:

Ingrid was acutely aware that she would soon have to leave her home to live in a memory care facility. Overwhelmed by grief and fear, Ingrid was sobbing as I sat down beside her. Coming alongside her in this time of personal crisis was an intangible expression of *Gifts*, known as "the gift of presence." As she sobbed, I gently rubbed her back (expressing *Physical Touch*). I said little, except to address her feeling of being rejected by her family. Softly, I spoke *Words of Affirmation:* "Your husband and daughter love you. You are so loved." She continued to sob, and I consoled her this way for perhaps half an hour.

When Ingrid's husband came and I stood to leave, Ingrid accepted my hug (*Physical Touch* again). I had no further expectations because Alzheimer's increasingly robs a person of the ability to "love you back." So I was surprised when this grieving woman with advanced dementia, for whom English was a second language, now spoke directly to me. With emotion, she said haltingly, "You. Are . . . *wonderful.*" Clearly, the combination of

Gifts, Physical Touch, and *Words of Affirmation* had communicated love to Ingrid!

Even in late dementia, people are still emotionally alive.

REFLECTIONS ON *LOVE LANGUAGES*

Note below some ways you can express each of the five love languages to the person for whom you provide care.

Physical Touch

Quality Moments

Gifts

Words of Affirmation

Acts of Kindness

For more ideas about how to use the five love languages with those who have Alzheimer's, see Appendix A (40 Ways to Say "I Love You") in *Keeping Love Alive as Memories Fade: The 5 Love Languages and the Alzheimer's Journey* (Northfield, 2016).

My journal . . .

Forgotten

Even if these forget . . .
ISAIAH 49:16A (CSB)

For Alex, the dreaded moment had finally arrived. The love of his life, his bride of nearly fifty years, looked at him with pleading eyes and asked, "Who are you?" For a few seconds, Alex could not breathe. As the meaning of her question sank into his heart, he did not even try to hold back the hot tears that sprang to his eyes. He struggled to grasp the unthinkable: Holly, the only woman he had ever loved, no longer remembered who he was.

Meredith and Macy, the couple's grown daughters, were equally devastated when it became clear that their mother no longer recognized them either. Each daughter felt that prior to Alzheimer's disease, Holly had truly been her lifelong best friend. Now the daughters grieved that the mother who had given birth to them, nourished them from her own body, and lovingly nurtured them to adulthood considered them strangers.

Like Alex and his daughters, many people recall the day that their loved one forgot them as one of the most painful days of their lives. When dementia erases the identity of one person from the mind of another, the forgotten person may experience a flood of emotions. Even when they know that the disease, not their loved one, is responsible, they may still suddenly feel alone or abandoned, rejected, angry, grieved, or many other things.

Have you been forgotten by a person with dementia? Take comfort, child of God, in the absolute certainty that you can never be forgotten by your heavenly Father. The sovereign God of the universe is incapable of forgetting, and you, His precious child, are always in His sight. His promise to the people of ancient Jerusalem is ours as well. You are, as they were, tattooed onto the very palms of His hands. He will never take His eyes off you, and He will never forget you.

Can a woman forget her nursing child,
or lack compassion for the child of her womb?
Even if these forget, yet I will not forget you.
Look, I have inscribed you on the palms of my hands . . .

ISAIAH 49:15–16a (csb)

REFLECTIONS ON *FORGOTTEN*

If your loved one has forgotten you, describe your feelings about this. If your loved one still remembers you, describe your feelings as you anticipate the day you may be forgotten.

If you have never done so before, write or speak to God about these feelings.

Circle the words in Isaiah 49:15–16a (csb) that are most meaningful to you. Describe below why these words are significant to you.

Can a woman forget her nursing child,
or lack compassion for the child of her womb?
Even if these forget, yet I will not forget you.
Look, I have inscribed you on the palms of my hands . . .

My journal . . .

Day 24

Life: It's So Daily

Praise be to the Lord, to God our Savior,
who daily bears our burdens.

PSALM 68:19 (NIV)

O*ne day at a time.* You've probably heard this phrase in many contexts. People struggling to overcome an addiction think about maintaining their sobriety one day at a time. The idea is that instead of focusing on the overwhelming goal of staying sober for the rest of their lives, they focus only on staying sober for the next twenty-four hours. This realistic goal is far less intimidating.

Misty's "one day at a time" is a little different. As the mother of five small children, Misty's days often consist of diapering, drying tears, wiping runny noses, and picking up toys over and over. Mothering her tribe of five is, she said, "so daily."

Gregg, the caregiver for his wife who has Alzheimer's, reflected on what he learned about "daily" during a difficult time in the past. He said, "Some of the things that

119

helped me get through that time have helped me get through this time of caregiving. One is that *just for today, just this day, right now in this day, this is good enough.*"

Living "one day at a time" is clearly God's design for us. A focus on what is *daily* appears throughout the Scriptures. When the Israelites were in the wilderness, "the LORD said to Moses, 'I will rain down bread from heaven for you. The people are to go out **each day** and gather enough for **that day**.'"[1] Similarly, Jesus taught the disciples to pray, "Give us **this day** our **daily** bread."[2] The writer of Hebrews tells us to "encourage each other **daily**, while it is still called **today** . . ."[3] Paul wrote to the Corinthian church, "Then, besides all this, I have the **daily** burden of my concern for all the churches."[4]

Whether we are trying to beat an addiction, caring for small children, or caring, as you are, for a person with dementia, we all travel through life in the same way: one day at a time. No one can relive a day that is past or fast-forward to one that is yet future. We are all bound by time; the only day anyone can live is the one called "today." For all of us, life is indeed *daily.*

As you carry out today's daily caregiving tasks, allow the Lord to walk with you and to carry for you anything that feels like a burden.

The only day anyone can live in is the one called "today."

REFLECTIONS ON *LIFE: IT'S SO DAILY*

Why do you think God designed our lives to be lived in the twenty-four-hour increments we call "days"?

When you focus your thoughts on the past or on the future, how does that affect your experience of today?

My journal . . .

Laughter

A cheerful heart is good medicine, but a crushed spirit dries up the bones.

PROVERBS 17:22 (NIV)

In an article about frontotemporal dementia (FTD), Comedy Central producer Nicole Savini wrote, "FTD is not funny. But that doesn't mean there's nothing to laugh about." She shared how her quick-witted father got his wife, who has FTD, to laugh: *On a recent trip, my mother told my father that she was looking out for dead animals on the side of the road. Rather than worry about why my mom said something so out of character, my dad quickly responded, "Oh, hon, I didn't realize you were so hungry." She thought that was very funny.*[1]

"There are some things that are just so funny, you have to laugh at them," said Sarah, a full-time Alzheimer's caregiver for her husband. She described how her husband had gone to change out of his church clothes and came back wearing, along with his black socks and dress shoes, a pair of Sarah's capri pants. "How he got them on

I don't know!" she said. "I really wasn't laughing *at* him; I was kind of laughing *with* him."[2]

By God's design, laughter boosts both physical and emotional health. Its many positive effects on well-being can strengthen your resiliency and help you cope better with the challenges of caregiving. Experts say that laughter:[3, 4]

- strengthens the immune system by increasing antibodies
- relaxes muscles throughout the body
- reduces tension, anxiety, and stress
- lowers bad cholesterol and elevates good cholesterol
- increases blood vessel elasticity
- increases energy
- helps prevent heart disease
- improves social connections
- shifts perspective in a positive direction

These physical and mental health benefits underscore what King Solomon wrote around 900 BC: "A cheerful heart is good medicine . . ." (Proverbs 17:22a NIV). Or, to say that another way, being cheerful helps keep you healthy. If this wisest man of all were alive today, Solomon might even agree that laughter is indeed "the best medicine" and prescribe a daily double dose of it for stressed-out caregivers. Laughter counteracts the effects of stress by stopping the release of the stress hormone, cortisol, and triggering the release of dopamine, which has a calming, anxiety-relieving effect.[5]

At least once a day, look away from the duties and challenges of caregiving and find something that makes you laugh. Stay in close touch with your most upbeat Christian friends. Look for funny books, movies, and internet videos. Even when those things can't be found, laugh anyway. Your body can't tell the difference between genuine and "fake" laughter. The benefits of laughter accrue regardless of *why* you are laughing. So, today and every day, go ahead and laugh—because it's really good for you!

Dementia is not funny. But that doesn't mean there's nothing to laugh about.

REFLECTIONS ON *LAUGHTER*

If the responsibilities of caregiving have put a damper on your sense of humor, how can you bring some laughter back into your life each day?

What do the built-in health benefits of laughter tell you about God? About His love and concern for you?

My journal . . .

_____

_____

_____

_____

_____

Paraclete (The Helper Jesus Sent)

*God is not unjust; he will not forget your work
and the love you have shown him as you have helped
his people and continue to help them.*

HEBREWS 6:10 (NIV)

In the book of John, Jesus speaks four times of an "Advocate" He will send to His disciples after He returns to heaven.[1] He said that this advocate would be with them forever, would help them, teach them, and bring to their remembrance everything He had told them. In each of these verses, the Greek word for advocate is *parakletos*.[2] This advocate of whom Christ speaks, the Paraclete, is the Holy Spirit.

One preacher shed light on the Holy Spirit's role when he described the role of an ancient paraclete in a sermon:

> *It was the custom, before the ancient tribunals, for the parties to appear in court, attended by one or more of their most powerful and influential friends, who*

were called "paracletes"... persons who, prompted
by affection, were disposed to stand by their friend;
and persons in whose knowledge, wisdom, and truth
the individual having the cause had confidence. These
paracletes ... stood by them in the court, giving them
advice, and speaking in their behalf when it was
necessary. Jesus had been the Paraclete of His disciples
while He was with them ... But He was to cease to
be their Paraclete on earth; and therefore, knowing
how much they needed such a patron and adviser,
and monitor and helper, He says, "I will pray to the
Father, and He will send you another Paraclete."[3]

Our Paraclete, the Holy Spirit, is also called Comforter, Helper, Intercessor, Counselor, Strengthener, Standby, and Spirit of Truth. Just as the Holy Spirit is all these things to us, His modern-day disciples, so are caregivers to those in their care. In your caregiving, you are never more God-like than when you emulate the Paraclete—advocating, comforting, helping, and interceding on behalf of the person in your care. In day-to-day life, caregivers demonstrate this in ordinary ways that are expressions of their love. Speaking to the members of his caregiver support group, Troy pointed this out. He said, "We show our love by trying to support them, by advocating for them at the doctor's office, by making sure they are dressed properly before they leave."

In a hundred other ways that Troy did not mention, caregivers act as "paracletes" for the person in their care. Advocating for this loved one is important work. God sees, and will one day reward all that you do.

Advocating for the person in your care is important work.

REFLECTIONS ON *PARACLETE*

Describe how you act as a "paraclete" for the person in your care (just as the Holy Spirit works on your behalf) in each of these roles:

Advocate

Comforter

Helper

Intercessor

Counselor

Strengthener

Standby

My journal . . .

Christ-Following

As the burdens of caregiving and senescence (the process of growing older) loom larger over time, caregivers who dismissed "religion" in their younger years may now yearn for a genuine connection with God. If this is true of you, consider why so many sincere Christ-followers don't describe Christianity as a religion. Instead, they speak more personally, referring to it as "a relationship." Specifically, it's a *love* relationship with the person, Jesus. It is the individual believer's love relationship with their Savior that sets Christianity apart from the religions of the world.

Singer/songwriter Jason Gray shed light on this difference between Christianity and other religions in his aptly titled song, "More Like Falling in Love." He told Kevin Davis, who interviewed Gray about the song, "I believe Jesus came to give us more than just better information about who God is. I believe He came to give us a relationship with God. At its most basic level, the story of Christianity is a love story between God and man."

Davis commented, "This song provides a real life picture of the difference between dead religion and a vibrant relationship with Christ, where faith can either be a burdensome, obligatory, passionless ideology or a response to love . . . "[1]

Be assured of this: God is no more interested in "burdensome, obligatory, passionless" religion than we are! Instead, He longs for us to respond to His love. If you have reached a point in your life where you would like to seriously explore, re-explore, or deepen your love relationship with God, here are two good places to start:

http://www.jesus.org
http://powertochange.com

We love because he first loved us.

1 JOHN 4:19 (CSB)

Christianity is a love story between God and man.

REFLECTIONS ON *CHRIST-FOLLOWING*

Would you say your faith is "more like falling in love" or more like something else?

If you would like a deeper connection with God, express that to Him aloud or in writing below. He is listening!

My journal . . .

Weary?

*It is in vain that you rise up early and go late to rest,
eating the bread of anxious toil; for he gives
to his beloved sleep.*

PSALM 127:2 (esv)

Alzheimer's disease or another dementia may change a person's sleep patterns. If the person for whom you provide care isn't sleeping well, it can impact your sleep too. You may be awakened by the other person's nighttime activity or verbal outbursts, or you may lie awake worrying about what may happen if he or she wanders during the night. If so, perhaps you arise weary each morning, struggling to find energy to meet the challenges of the new day.

If you often feel weary, especially in the morning, maybe you can relate to the hardworking, weary man, Jacob. Yes, we're talking about *that* Jacob—the one who deceived his father and cheated his brother out of his birthright. To escape his brother's wrath, Jacob fled to the kingdom of Paddan Aram. There, you may recall,

Jacob worked for twenty years diligently tending sheep and goats for a most unappreciative employer, his father-in-law, Laban. Jacob summarized the weariness of those years when he said, "There I was: by day the heat consumed me, and the cold by night, and my sleep fled from my eyes" (Genesis 31:40 ESV).

Jacob finally solved his sleep problem (and his in-law problem as well) by relocating his family to a place called Succoth, which means "shelters." It is vital for you to also solve the problems that disrupt your sleep. A poor night's sleep can leave you feeling depressed, cause attention and memory problems, increase your daytime sleepiness, and put you at risk for nighttime falls. Because of your caregiving responsibilities, adequate sleep is not a luxury; it's an insurance policy that will help you continue to provide quality care for your loved one.

A good first step toward better sleep is to improve nighttime safety for the person with dementia. The National Institute on Aging (NIA) suggests:[1]

- Make sure the floor is clear of objects.
- Lock up any medicines.
- Attach grab bars in the bathroom.
- Place a gate across the stairs.

You may also want to consider hiring an overnight caregiver to relieve you of your duties so you can sleep. If finances do not permit this, perhaps friends or relatives can take turns providing nighttime care or afternoon care so you can at least nap.

Be assured that restful sleep is indeed God's desire for you. After all, He created the human body and its requirements for sleep. Remember that while you sleep, God remains vigilant: "Behold, He who keeps Israel will neither slumber nor sleep" (Psalm 121:4 ESV).

For caregivers, sleep is not a luxury; it's an insurance policy that helps ensure quality care for the person with dementia.

REFLECTIONS ON *WEARY?*

How does Psalm 127:2 apply to your current circumstances and your attitude about sleep?

If a good night's sleep seems like a luxury that is out of your reach, prayerfully brainstorm below some ideas about how to solve the issues that are robbing you of sleep.

My journal . . .

Contentment: Paul's Secret

*I have learned to be content in whatever
circumstances I find myself.*

PHILIPPIANS 4:11B (CSB)

Philippians 4:11–13 is one of the most well-known New Testament passages. It sets forth the beloved apostle Paul's personal perspective on contentment:

> *. . . I have learned how to get along happily whether I have much or little. I know how to live on almost nothing or with everything. I have learned the secret of contentment in every situation, whether it be a full stomach or hunger, plenty or want; for I can do everything God asks me to with the help of Christ who gives me the strength and power.* (TLB)

In these verses, the words "plenty" and "want" underscore for us that Paul's contentment was truly independent of his circumstances. While we modern believers admire such unflappable contentment and may even openly aspire to it, it can be an awfully difficult mindset for us to embrace. In times of "want," with barely enough to meet our needs, we tend to yearn for more money to fix our situation. In times of "plenty," with more than enough to relieve our needs, we (Americans in particular) tend to yearn for more stuff.

How did Paul do it?

In his commentary on Philippians 4, John Darby answers this question. He writes, "Christ had always been faithful to [Paul], had brought him through so many difficulties and through so many seasons of prosperity, that he had learnt to trust in Him, and not in circumstances."[1] In his early life, Paul enjoyed "seasons of prosperity" due to his social status and the abundance of his station in life. He was a Pharisee, a Roman citizen, well educated under the famous rabbi Gamaliel, and fluent in both Greek and Hebrew. He was so well respected that the rabbinical authorities authorized him to persecute Christians.[2, 3] After his conversion to Christ, life radically changed for Paul. The price he paid for proclaiming Christ was very high: he was imprisoned, beaten, stoned, whipped, shipwrecked, and suffered sleepless nights, hunger, thirst, and exposure to cold due to lack of proper clothing.[4] Thus, Paul was supremely well qualified to say, "I know how to live on almost nothing or with everything" (TLB). By the time he wrote Philippians,

Paul had truly come to the place in his life where his attitude could not be altered by circumstances. Whether times were good or bad, Paul faced each circumstance in exactly the same way: with contentment through the power of Christ.

In your difficult work as a caregiver, that same power of Christ is available to you. No matter how caregiving impacts your lifestyle, finances, relationships, health, or your future, the same power of Christ that carried Paul can carry you. There is no circumstance, no challenge, and no moment in which you cannot be, as Paul was, contented in Christ. Paul's "secret" belongs to you and to all of us as well: "I am able to do all things through him who strengthens me" (Philippians 4:13 CSB).

Paul's contentment was independent
of his circumstances.

REFLECTIONS ON
CONTENTMENT: PAUL'S SECRET

How did Paul define contentment?

Based on this definition, how contented are you?

In the verse above, what is the significance of the word *learned* in Paul's statement, "I have learned to be content in whatever circumstances I find myself"?

My journal . . .

God's Masterpiece

For we are God's masterpiece . . .

EPHESIANS 2:10

MASTERPIECE: a work done with extraordinary skill;
especially: a supreme intellectual or artistic achievement
(merriam-webster.com)

The Bible says that you are God's masterpiece. According to the definition above, as the living handiwork of God, you are His supreme achievement. Because you are a reflection of your Creator, it is your privilege to serve as His hands and feet on this earth. In other words, God has work for you to do! This is the message of Ephesians 2:10—"For we are God's masterpiece. He has created us anew in Christ Jesus, so we can do the good things he planned for us long ago." The New International Version calls these good things "good works."

If you are struggling to relate this verse to your life, maybe it's because your current "good works"—the ones you do in the daily grind of caregiving—are not the ones you would like to be doing at this time in your life. Are you perhaps even disappointed that God didn't have a better job in mind for you, His masterpiece? If so, Henry Blackaby, author of the book *Experiencing God*, has some encouragement for you: "Remain faithful in what He has told you to do, no matter how small or seemingly insignificant it may appear. God knows what He is doing. Focus on deepening your communion with God, and out of that fellowship will inevitably flow effective service for God."[1]

Do you agree with Blackaby's counsel but find that you're not quite "there" yet? If so, don't be too hard on yourself. It takes a while to adjust to the idea of being a caregiver. Few people expect to spend part of their lives caring for a family member with dementia. If caregiving wasn't on your original bucket list, you will certainly understand how Sandra felt when her husband was diagnosed with early-onset Alzheimer's disease. She admitted,

> *In the beginning, I was kicking and screaming as a caregiver. It's not my modus operandi—I am not a caring, demonstrative kind of person. So, when we first got the diagnosis I was full throttle into finding places that could care for him or support groups that we could both go to. It was a chore. I was stressed. I felt very put upon and I just wanted to really get my career back on track. I am not proud of that; it's just how I was at the beginning of caregiving.*

Months later, a crisis related to her husband's care completely changed Sandra's point of view. She said, "I went from being a reluctant caregiver to being full-in."[2]

Sarah also went through a period of adjustment. She had been her husband's caregiver for six years when she reflected with satisfaction, "God gives different people different gifts. You stop and think about it, isn't this the gift that He gave me, for caring? I can't imagine myself doing anything else in my life right now except taking care of Bob."[3]

If your loved one is in the beginning stages of dementia, you may still be, as Sandra initially was, "kicking and screaming as a caregiver." If you have been a caregiver for a long time, you may have come to the same place as Sarah, unable to imagine yourself apart from your caregiving role. No matter where you are on the "caregiving acceptance continuum," never lose sight of the fact that you are also God's masterpiece. This means your life is, and will always be, both precious to God and supremely purposeful as you tend to the "good works" He has asked you to do.

Your life is both precious to God and supremely purposeful.

REFLECTIONS ON *GOD'S MASTERPIECE*

What does it mean to you to be "God's Masterpiece"?

How do you feel about the idea that caregiving is one of the "good works" that God planned for you long ago?

My journal . . .

Day 31

Caregiving: The Movie

Whatever you do, work at it with all your heart,
as working for the Lord, not for human masters, since you
know that you will receive an inheritance from the Lord as a
reward. It is the Lord Christ you are serving.

COLOSSIANS 3:23–24 (NIV)

One evening, a friend and I watched *Until Forever,* a movie based on the true story of Michael and Michelle Boyum, a young Minnesota couple. Michael, Michelle, and their families relied on their faith in Christ for strength and endurance throughout Michael's ordeal with a rare form of leukemia. This beautifully written and well-acted movie touched my heart very deeply and moved me to tears.

The movie put me in a pensive frame of mind. I thought about those who had surrounded these young people with their presence and prayers during their time of suffering; how would Michael and Michelle have fared without this cocoon of love around them? I thought about those who had both the God-given talent and the vision to make their story into a movie. Because many people had yielded their talents to God, I was blessed by this story, and am now writing about its impact on me. These talented people did what they did because of their faith in God. All along, God intended to bring great good from the sadness and suffering of two people who loved Him deeply. Such are the mysterious ways of God, who sometimes showcases His extravagant love through circumstances we would never choose.

As I reflected on these things, I also thought of you, a Christ-follower unwittingly cast in the role of "caregiver" in an unfolding drama of dementia. Because no filmmaker will probably make a movie about your life, few people will ever know what you do faithfully, day in and day out. But in the theater of heaven, your story is a big hit. God, your biggest fan, intently watches in real time each day as you serve and love and sacrifice for the person in your care. He knows the meaning of every expression that crosses your face, and He reads your heart as well, so He knows you grow weary and are sometimes not "into" doing what needs to be done. When you do it anyway, from the balcony of heaven He rejoices and applauds. He knows you are not acting, and He loves the "movie" of your life that He is watching. He knows too that a great reward awaits you—one far more precious and eternal than any Hollywood Oscar.

REFLECTIONS ON *CAREGIVING: THE MOVIE*

What comes to your mind as you read Colossians 3:23–24?

Why do you think God sometimes showcases His extravagant love in circumstances we would never choose?

My journal . . .

Hangry

Then the Angel of the Lord came again and touched (Elijah) and said, "Get up and eat some more, for there is a long journey ahead of you." So he got up and ate and drank, and the food gave him enough strength to travel forty days and forty nights to Mount Horeb, the mountain of God.

1 KINGS 19:7–8 (TLB)

Did you think, "There's a mistake in that title"? There's no mistake! *Hangry* is a portmanteau—a word created by blending two or more other words. (More common portmanteaus are *smog*, a blend of *smoke* and *fog*, and *brunch*, a blend of *breakfast* and *lunch*.)

Hangry is an adjective that has only been around since the 1990s. It's a blend of the words *hungry* and *angry*. If you have ever felt grumpy and irritable after missing a meal, you've been hangry. We've all seen the effects of "hanger." That's why we laugh when we see a T-shirt that says, "Just hand over the chocolate and no one gets hurt." Hangry caregivers, however, are no laughing matter.

Many caregivers focus so much time and attention on the person in their care that they do not take the time to cook or to ensure that they are eating healthfully. They may skip meals or eat mostly junk food or fast food. In other words, they neglect their body's basic need for proper nourishment.

Not everyone who is hungry or undernourished gets hangry. But for many people, when hunger causes blood sugar to drop, the result is a short emotional fuse. Experts also say that low blood sugar can trigger the release of adrenalin and cortisol, the "fight-or-flight" hormones. Simple tasks seem more difficult, and we may more easily snap at people who irritate us. The danger for hangry caregivers, of course, is lashing out, verbally or physically, at the person in their care.

If you are a caregiver with a history of addiction, you may already realize how wise it is to pay attention to feelings of hunger. Hunger is one component of the acronym HALT—Hunger, Anger, Loneliness, Tiredness. Addiction counselors say that whenever a person in recovery is hungry, angry, lonely, or tired, they don't cope as well and there is greater potential for relapse. HALT is a good reminder for all caregivers: when feelings of hunger occur, push the pause button and take care of yourself by eating something nourishing.

The way to avoid ever becoming hangry, of course, is

to eat regularly and to nourish your body with well-balanced meals and healthy snacks. Ideally, both you and the person in your care should eat some healthy morsel every three hours. Eating well is not a luxury for caregivers; it is a necessity. Well-nourished caregivers won't get hangry, which means they will be more likely to feel better, think better, and exhibit more Christlike kindness and patience toward the person with dementia.

Eating well is not a luxury for caregivers; it is a necessity.

REFLECTIONS ON *HANGRY*

Do you think of regular meals and nutritious snacks as a luxury, a necessity, or as unimportant?

In your own life, do you detect a connection between hunger and anger?

If you are a person who gets "hangry," how can you establish more regular and healthful eating habits?

My journal . . .

Day 33

Pruning

I am the true vine, and my Father is the gardener.
He cuts off every branch in me that bears no fruit, while
every branch that does bear fruit he prunes so that it
will be even more fruitful.

JOHN 15:1–2 (NIV)

How has caregiving changed you? What has caregiving taught you about yourself? When I asked some caregivers to answer these questions, several of their responses centered around three common themes.

Increased Patience

"I have become more patient, certainly not as much as I aspire to be, but I have improved."

"I have learned to be more patient and caring. I traded my patients for patience" (from a retired physician).

Living in the Present

"I have learned more about living in *this* moment . . . to laugh, to remember, to pause and look at a beautiful sunset—these are finite pleasures and they must be enjoyed in this 'now' rather than postponed for a more convenient time."

"Live in the now rather than the past or the future."

Mastering New Tasks

Self-efficacy is one's belief about their own ability to succeed or accomplish tasks. As one's spouse or parent loses the ability to do certain things, caregivers must often step in and learn how to do those tasks. Some people noted that mastering new tasks had increased their self-efficacy.

"I can do things I didn't know I could. I am stronger than I thought."

"I've learned how to do almost anything my husband used to do around the house."

Caregiving experiences that are powerful enough to increase patience, raise self-efficacy, or cause us to savor the present moment may qualify as events the Bible calls "pruning." Just as cutting back parts of a plant eventually causes more fruitful growth, spiritual pruning has a similar result in our lives. But as shrubs, rosebushes, and many Christians can testify, pruning is not a pleasant experience! Christians are faithfully pruned by God, not because He delights in our discomfort, but because He wants us to be more fruitful.

God's hand is seen in the pruning outcomes above: patience is a fruit of the Spirit;[1] living in the present is certainly God's will;[2] and for believers, self-efficacy is never apart from "Christ-efficacy," as Paul's words remind us: "I can do all things through him who strengthens me."[3] Pruning is not limited to these three categories, however. As you may already have discovered, God customizes His pruning to the individual believer. Are you being pruned by the caregiving experience? Hold on to the truth that while pruning is painful, any area of your life that the Master Gardener prunes will not only bear more fruit, but more excellent fruit.

God customizes His pruning to the individual believer.

REFLECTIONS ON *PRUNING*

How is the experience of caregiving pruning you?

What does God's commitment to pruning you tell you
about His love and concern for you?

My journal . . .

_____

_____

_____

_____

_____

_____

_____

_____

_____

Day 34

Faithfulness

... when the Holy Spirit controls our lives he will produce this kind of fruit in us: love, joy, peace, patience, kindness, goodness, **faithfulness,** *gentleness and self-control .*

GALATIANS 5:22–23 (TLB)

Troy is well acquainted with the pressures that dementia places on a marriage. Before his wife was diagnosed, her inexplicable and increasingly bizarre behaviors had put so much strain on their relationship that Troy finally decided to separate from her. He had a change of heart, however, when the explanation for her odd behaviors was finally revealed: early-onset Alzheimer's disease. Troy now understood that the dramatic changes in his wife's personality were not really "her," but the disease that was taking hold of her. He returned to his wife with a softer heart and a renewed commitment to loving and caring for her. He said, "Short of unfaithfulness, there is probably no stronger test of marital love than Alzheimer's disease."[1]

Rick is also familiar with this test of marital love. He

had been married to Stephanie for only a few years when she was diagnosed with early-onset Alzheimer's. Because the marriage was new and his wife was still young, Rick's first thought was to call Stephanie's parents and say, "Your daughter is seriously ill. I can't handle it. Can you come and get her?" However, like Troy, Rick had a change of heart. Now he says, "I'm so glad I never followed through on my initial thoughts of perhaps hanging it up."[2]

Many spouse caregivers entertain thoughts of separation or divorce at some point during the Alzheimer's journey. While it's only human to want to escape an emotionally painful, physically exhausting situation, Troy, Rick, and others have chosen to remain faithful to the marriage vows they and their spouses had made before God.

Gracie said, "Each day I am challenged to honor this marriage, not because I want to, but because I have great trust in and love for God who wants to use this for my good, refining me and making me more like Him. God wants me to love my husband as He loves him. This is not always easy."

By continually choosing to hang in there, Troy, Rick, and Gracie are living demonstrations of *faithfulness.* Faithfulness means *loyalty* or *steadfast adherence to a promise.* Faithfulness is an expression of the character of God that is reproduced by the Holy Spirit in the lives of surrendered believers. Thus, a faithful man or woman both honors God and displays His character. While faithfulness is always the honorable path, it's not always the easy path. As missionary Elisabeth Elliot has said, however, "The secret to enduring is Christ in me, not me in a different set of circumstances."

With the help of Christ, you can continue to be a faithful caregiver!

> The secret to enduring is Christ in me,
> not me in a different set of circumstances.
> —ELISABETH ELLIOT

REFLECTIONS ON *FAITHFULNESS*

Based on the definition below, how do you currently express faithfulness to the person for whom you provide care?

Faithfulness means loyalty or the steadfast adherence to a promise. Faithfulness is an expression of the character of God that is reproduced by the Holy Spirit in the lives of surrendered believers.

What does the Elisabeth Elliot quote mean to you?

My journal . . .

In Their Shoes

Finally, all of you should be of one mind. Sympathize with each other. Love each other as brothers and sisters. Be tender-hearted, and keep a humble attitude.

1 PETER 3:8

Penny and her friend Sarah have observed their husbands' discouragement over losing some of their abilities due to Alzheimer's disease. Penny's husband tells her that he is now "Mr. Useless." Sarah's husband says, "I'm just so stupid. I'm not good for anybody." Penny said with sadness, "We don't know what that feels like inside of them."[1]

Lately, Penny has also been wondering how her husband feels about something else. Sometimes, to cope with the pressures of caregiving, Penny admits, "I just try to go numb." She mused, "I wonder what it feels like to him, how he might sense that."

One younger caregiver whose wife has early-onset Alzheimer's disease said, "I would like for people when they read this to take some time to think, and put themselves in the body or in the mind of the person who has the disease. When I think about this from my wife's perspective, it makes me just cherish her that much more, knowing what she's going through and what she does every day just to try to survive, just to walk. Put yourself in their shoes."

These caregivers have great empathy for their spouses. Empathy is often confused with sympathy. *Dictionary.com* distinguishes between these two terms: *"sympathy* is feeling compassion, sorrow, or pity for the hardships that another person encounters, while *empathy* is putting yourself in the shoes of another."[2]

One psychologist explained, "Empathy means being able to step into someone else's shoes and then step out of them again. What happens when we inhabit their shoes is supposed to give us an understanding of their experience, their feelings and their point of view."[3]

Empathizing with a demented person can increase your insight about how to best respond to their behaviors and emotions. Experts say that anyone can become more empathetic by paying attention to three things,[4] each of which can help caregivers connect better to a person with dementia:

- Focus your attention on the person's facial and eye expressions, body language, and gestures, as these are all clues about their emotional state.

- Practice listening to your own tone of voice. It is especially important to speak calmly to those with dementia, striving to have warmth in your voice. In the later stages of dementia, even if a person cannot respond to you, they can still sense empathy in your tone.

- Practice "cognitive empathy." This means that even when you truly don't feel what the person is feeling, you do still intellectually understand their need for empathy. In these instances, you can choose to communicate empathy by letting the person know that you understand and care about what they are experiencing.

As you become more empathetic toward the person in your care, you become a wider channel for God's love to flow from your heart to theirs.

Even if a person cannot respond to you, they can still sense empathy in your tone.

Would you rather experience sympathy or empathy from others?

How might empathizing with a demented person give you a better understanding of their behaviors and emotions?

My journal . . .

Shalom

You keep him in perfect peace whose mind is stayed
on you, because he trusts in you.

ISAIAH 26:3 (ESV)

S halom! The world over, people know that this Hebrew word means *peace.* You may have used this
word yourself, as many people do, to greet a friend who
is arriving or to say goodbye to one who is leaving. The
true meaning of shalom, however, is much richer than
these common uses of the word.

The deeper meaning of shalom centers on the idea of
completeness. In the truest sense of the word, shalom
means *complete peace*: a sense of well-being, wholeness,
contentment, security, harmony, and prosperity. It not
only means the absence of war, but also a tranquil, safe,
and orderly personal life that is free of agitation and discord. Shalom means that one is at peace within oneself,
with those in the family and community, and at peace
with God.

The human heart was made for shalom. Yet, in our

chaotic, politically volatile, stressful, uncertain world, *external* shalom is rare and fleeting. If the person for whom you provide care is prone to sundowning, agitation, aggression, or hallucinations, even your home environment may not be peaceful. However, *internal* shalom *can* be found—but only by followers of Jesus, the Messiah. He is the "Prince of Peace" who was foretold by the prophet Isaiah.[1] Paul wrote, ". . . God cleared a path for everything to come to him—all things in heaven and on earth—for Christ's death on the cross has made peace with God for all by his blood."[2] All who accept His shed blood as payment for their sins have shalom with God, beginning at that moment and lasting forever. This peace with God, through the power of the Holy Spirit, also enables believers to experience the same internal peace that exists in Christ's own inner being (". . . the fruit of the Spirit is love, joy, **peace**. . ." (Galatians 5:22 CSB).

When you and I one day step from this earthly life into eternity, we will finally experience the fulfillment of complete shalom, both internally and externally in the sinless perfection of heaven. While we still abide here on earth, our experience of inner shalom depends upon the extent to which we are able to trust in and focus our minds on *Jehovah-Shalom* ("The LORD is peace"), God Himself (Judges 6:24 CSB).

Your home environment may not be peaceful—but if you are a follower of Christ, you can find internal shalom.

REFLECTIONS ON *SHALOM*

According to Isaiah 26:3, what is the secret to experiencing internal shalom?

My journal . . .

Bitter or Better?

No matter what happens, always be thankful, for this is God's will for you who belong to Christ Jesus.

1 THESSALONIANS 5:18 (TLB)

When a severe famine came upon Israel, Elimelech, his wife, Naomi, and their two sons moved from the town of Bethlehem to the country of Moab. After the family was settled in this foreign land, Elimelech passed away, a heartbreaking loss for Naomi and her sons, Mahlon and Chilion. The widow and her fatherless sons remained in Moab and both sons married Moabite women. About ten years later, Naomi's heart was broken a second time when, unbelievably, both of her sons passed away.

Naomi and her two daughters-in-law decided to move back to Israel because the famine was now over. On the road to Israel, Naomi pleaded with the two young women to go back to their own families. She told them, "Things are far more bitter for me than for you, because the LORD himself has raised his fist against me." The three wept together, and one daughter-in-law kissed

Naomi goodbye and returned to her people. The other daughter-in-law, Ruth, traveled on with Naomi.

Naomi's use of the word "bitter" reveals how deeply the deaths of her husband and sons had impacted her. By the time she arrived in Bethlehem, bitterness had become her identity. She no longer wanted to be called Naomi, which means *sweet* or *pleasant*. She now wanted to be known as Mara, which means *bitter*.

The Bible reports, "When they came to Bethlehem, the entire town was excited by their arrival. 'Is it really Naomi?' the women asked. 'Don't call me Naomi,' she responded. 'Instead, call me Mara, for the Almighty has made life very bitter for me. I went away full, but the Lord has brought me home empty. Why call me Naomi when the Lord has caused me to suffer and the Almighty has sent such tragedy upon me?'" (Ruth 1:19–21)

God's goodness soon proved greater than Naomi's bitterness. The rest of the story chronicles how He provided for Naomi and Ruth through Boaz, a relative of Naomi's late husband. It also reveals the ultimate divine purpose for the painful circumstances that led Naomi and Ruth back to Bethlehem. Ruth married Boaz and the couple was blessed with a son whom they named Obed ("worshiper"). Obed grew up to become the father of Jesse, whose son was King David, the ancestor of Jesus the Christ (Ruth 4:16–17).

Today, we see this story in historical perspective. We now understand that Naomi's painful experiences paved the way for the birth of the Savior generations later. However, while Naomi was in the midst of her troubles and unable to see God's bigger plan, she allowed herself to become bitter. Perhaps you are experiencing a "Naomi moment" in your life right now. You may be in a difficult caregiving situation with no clue about God's ultimate purpose. Like Naomi, you have a choice to make. Will you allow your caregiving situation to make you bitter? Or will you allow it to make you better, believing that God's purposes are greater than what you can see?

Will you allow your caregiving situation to make you bitter or better?

REFLECTIONS ON *BITTER OR BETTER?*

Naomi said, "The LORD himself has raised his fist against me." Was she right?

How can you ensure that your caregiving journey makes you better instead of bitter?

My journal . . .

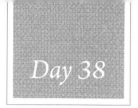

In the Potter's Hands

*This is the word that came to Jeremiah from
the LORD: "Go down to the potter's house, and
there I will give you my message."*

*So I went down to the potter's house, and I saw
him working at the wheel. But the pot he was shaping from
the clay was marred in his hands; so the potter formed it
into another pot, shaping it as seemed best to him.*

*Then the word of the LORD came to me. He said, "Can I not
do with you, Israel, as this potter does?" declares the LORD.*

*"Like clay in the hand of the potter, so are you
in my hand, Israel."*

JEREMIAH 18:1–6 (NIV)

The year was 1902. A very discouraged Adelaide Pollard was sitting in an evening prayer service when she heard an elderly woman say, "Lord, it doesn't matter what you bring into our lives—just have your way with us." These words resonated deeply with Adelaide. She had earnestly hoped to go to Africa as a missionary but had been unable to raise the funds that would make it possible.

Adelaide pondered the older woman's words in the light of Jeremiah 18:3–4. Later that evening at home, she penned four stanzas of verse that would later become the lyrics to the beloved hymn, "Have Thine Own Way, Lord."[1, 2]

Does that same Jeremiah passage speak to you today?

Do you feel like the clay on the potter's wheel, pressed down by the hand of God and being reshaped by Him? The caregiving experience may, in fact, be His hand turning your life "as seemed best to him." Though you may wonder *why*, as Adelaide did, if you are nonetheless willing to say, "Yes, Lord," let Adelaide's response to God become your prayer too:

> *Have Thine own way, Lord!*
> *Have Thine own way!*
> *Thou art the potter; I am the clay.*
> *Mold me and make me after Thy will,*
> *While I am waiting, yielded and still.*

Thou art the potter; I am the clay.

REFLECTIONS ON *IN THE POTTER'S HANDS*

What important point is God making to Israel in Jeremiah 18:1–6?

How does this same truth apply in your life?

My journal . . .

Bearing One Another's Burdens

He comforts us in all our troubles so that we can comfort others. When they are troubled, we will be able to give them the same comfort God has given us.

2 CORINTHIANS 1:4

Fred is the primary care partner for his wife, Michelle, who has Alzheimer's disease. He said, "I think knowledge is power. It has been very important to me to learn as much as I could about this disease."

One of Fred's most valued sources of information has been his caregiver support group. He explained, "My wife is still in the early stages. Another support group member said to me one time, 'When you hear us talk about our spouses being further along, and some of our trials, is that hard for you?'" Fred said he told her, "No, I find it very helpful to hear from all of you so that when I get to that point, I will have your words of wisdom."

Participating in a support group makes caregivers like Fred feel less alone. Because everyone in the group is dealing with similar issues, a support group offers a level of understanding and camaraderie that is hard to find elsewhere. Linda, a member of Fred's group, said, "People who haven't been around Alzheimer's don't understand what you are really going through." In the group, however, everyone understands. Another member of the group was emotional as she shared something with the group that she had not told anyone else. She chose to share it only within the group simply because, as she told them, "I don't have to explain it to you all."

Caregivers benefit from hearing each other's experiences and sharing caregiving tips and advice. This can occur in an organized support group or in an impromptu conversation. Among believers, there can be an even deeper connection as they comfort one another with Scripture and pray for each other. As believing caregivers reach out to each other, they fulfill part of their Christian mission: "Rejoice with those who rejoice, and weep with those who weep" (Romans 12:15 ESV); "Bear one another's burdens, and so fulfill the law of Christ" (Galatians 6:2 ESV).

Don't underestimate the value of connecting with other caregivers! You will learn from them and be encouraged by them. The lessons you have learned on your caregiving journey can also encourage and support others traveling the same road. As you engage with other caregivers and share both joys and struggles with them, you can find new purpose and meaning in caregiving. Your daily focus will no longer be limited to yourself and your loved one. It will expand to encompass a wider community of people whose daily lives are very much like yours. The role you can play in the lives of other caregivers may in fact be part of God's purpose for you in this season of your life.

Caregivers who open their lives to one another may find new meaning and purpose in their unexpected journey.

REFLECTIONS ON
BEARING ONE ANOTHER'S BURDENS

What kinds of support do you most need to receive from other caregivers?

What kinds of support can you offer to other caregivers?

My journal . . .

Day 40

Live in Peace

Let us therefore make every effort to do what leads to peace and to mutual edification.

ROMANS 14:19 (NIV)

Paul counsels us, "Do all that you can to live in peace with everyone" (Romans 12:18). If you live with a person who has Alzheimer's disease, you know that living "in peace" can require some extra-special effort.

To live peacefully with an Alzheimer's patient, one must choose to enter into their world. In this world, starting around the middle of the disease, facts and reason are sometimes trumped by the faulty thinking that arises from hallucinations or delusions. The way that caregivers and others respond to these false perceptions can either promote peace or invite discord.

Hallucinations

About 15 percent of those with Alzheimer's disease have hallucinations.[1] Hallucinations involve the senses: seeing, hearing, tasting, touching, or smelling something that isn't really there. Visual hallucinations are more common. Someone may misinterpret sensory information for many reasons, such as too much or too little light, shadows, and/or poor memory. When a person is having a hallucination, the way a caregiver responds can either help or hinder peace.

What hinders: Agnes tells you that she had lunch with her mother today and that her mother is a great cook. When you respond, "Your mother did not have lunch with you. She has been dead for thirty years!" Agnes begins to cry. Although you may have told her many times, because Agnes cannot remember that her mother is dead, she reacts as if she is hearing for the first time that her mother has died.

What helps: Enter into Agnes's world and play along. Ignore the fact that her mother is deceased and ask, "What did your mother cook for lunch today?" This is a kinder response that spares Agnes from grieving her mother's death over and over.

Delusions

About 70 percent of people with Alzheimer's experience delusions.[2] A delusion is the belief that something is true when it is not. A person experiencing a paranoid delusion may be suspicious, distrustful, or fearful. She may believe that someone is spying on her or has stolen her money, clothes, or a personal possession. She may respond with accusations of theft. As with hallucinations, a caregiver's response can either help or hinder peace.

What hinders: Clara can't find her pearl necklace. She shouts, "That girl next door took my necklace!" You try to reason with her, explaining that the neighbor has not been in the house, but she becomes more agitated. Next, you gently suggest that maybe she has misplaced the necklace, and this upsets her even more.

What helps: When a person is not thinking rationally, respond to the *feeling* they are expressing. Stating facts or attempting to reason with a delusional person may only inflame the situation. In the instance with Clara, the best approach would be to calmly say, "I know you really want to find your necklace. I will help you look for it." This supportive approach aligns with what she is feeling and avoids an argument about the facts.

It is easier to "live in peace" with someone who has Alzheimer's disease when you (1) join them in their world and (2) respond to their feelings rather than try to convince them of facts.

When a person with Alzheimer's is not thinking
rationally, respond to the feeling they are expressing.

REFLECTIONS ON *LIVE IN PEACE*

What are some ways you can "enter into the world" of the person for whom you provide care?

How difficult is it for you to respond to a person's feelings when they are not thinking in a rational way?

My journal . . .

Immanuel

"Look! The virgin will conceive a child!
She will give birth to a son,
and they will call him Immanuel,
which means 'God is with us.'"

MATTHEW 1:23

. . . the Holy Spirit who lives within us . . .

2 TIMOTHY 1:14

When Alzheimer's disease or another dementia begins to affect a person, loved ones may at first only sense that something is now "different." Relationships gradually grow distant as dementia weakens the emotional bonds that connect human beings to one another. Eventually, the person with the disease loses the ability to hold up his or her side of the relationship. As a relationship that was once emotionally equal becomes more and more one-sided, care *partners* become caregivers and their journey often becomes very lonely.

If you are a Christ-follower, however, while you may

feel lonely, it is certain that you are never *alone.*

The very name of your Lord Jesus is Immanuel, which means "God is with us."

God has always desired to be with His people. In Old Testament times, God the Holy Spirit was present on earth, manifesting Himself and His power at various times in various ways. When Jesus the Messiah was born, God the Son entered the world bodily, in human form. He walked and talked, ate, slept, and wept, just as those He created did then and do now. When Jesus returned to heaven He told His followers, "I will ask the Father, and he will give you another Counselor to be with you forever. He is the Spirit of truth. The world is unable to receive him because it doesn't see him or know him. But you do know him, because he remains with you and will be in you" (John 14:16–17 csb).

Wait—did you get that? Jesus was promising His disciples that one day the Holy Spirit would not only be *with* believers, but actually, literally, reside *within* all who are truly His. This promise was fulfilled on the day of Pentecost (Acts chapter 2). Since that day, the Holy Spirit has not just been with, but within, all true Christ followers.

If Christ is your Savior, the Holy Spirit lives in you and He will never leave you. Though the gulf between you and the person for whom you provide care is certain to widen, you can take great comfort in the knowledge that you will not be alone for one moment of your caregiving journey. You can continually rely upon, rest in, and be guided by the Holy Spirit's loving, faithful presence within you.

If you are God's child, you will not be alone for one moment of your caregiving journey.

REFLECTIONS ON *IMMANUEL*

Are you uncertain about the presence of Immanuel, "God with us," in your life?

If so, you can resolve your uncertainty. You can do what millions of others have already done: accept as payment for your personal sins what Jesus accomplished for you on the cross and invite Him to be your Savior. The moment you do this, your sins are forgiven and the Holy Spirit, "God with us," comes to live within you. If this is your desire, write below (or speak) your decision to God. (If you have already done this in the past, you may want to instead make your prayer an expression of thanks.)

My journal . . .

If you would like to remember today as the day you become a Christ-follower, write today's date here:

_____.

Day 42

Feelings and Moments

A man who is kind benefits himself,
but a cruel man hurts himself.

PROVERBS 11:17 (esv)

Have you ever wondered if being kind to a person with Alzheimer's really makes any difference? Has anyone ever asked you, "If he won't even remember that I was there, why should I visit?" Research done at the University of Iowa provides a powerful and encouraging answer to these questions.

Researchers asked two groups of people to watch twenty minutes of movie clips that evoked either happiness or sadness. One group had Alzheimer's; the other group did not. As expected, people laughed during the happy clips and were sorrowful and teary during the sad ones. Following the movies, everyone was tested to see what they remembered about what they had just seen. Not surprisingly, the people with Alzheimer's remembered less than the healthy people. One person didn't even recall seeing the movie clips.

Before and after the movies, both groups were also asked about their feelings. The amazing thing was, thirty minutes after the movies ended, when the people with Alzheimer's remembered little or nothing about what they had seen, their *feelings* of happiness or sadness persisted. Most interesting of all, the less a person remembered about the movies, the longer their feelings of happiness or sadness lasted.

The results of this study were published in the journal *Cognitive and Behavioral Neurology*. The investigators wrote:

> *The fact that these patients' feelings can persist, even in the absence of memory, highlights the need to avoid causing negative feelings and to try to induce positive feelings with frequent visits and social interactions, exercise, music, dance, jokes, and serving patients their favorite foods. Thus, our findings should empower caregivers by showing them that their actions toward patients really do matter and can significantly influence a patient's quality of life and subjective well-being.*[1]

In the words of one writer who reported on this study, the "inescapable message" of this research is that "caregivers have a profound influence—good or bad—on the emotional state of individuals with Alzheimer's disease."[2]

Thus, the two important takeaway messages for caregivers are:

1. Feelings, both positive and negative, persist after a person with dementia has forgotten the words or actions that sparked those feelings.

2. It is important to intentionally create positive feelings for people with Alzheimer's and, to the extent possible, to avoid creating negative feelings.

Keep in mind that as Alzheimer's disease progresses, people increasingly experience life only in *moments*. That is, they experience time less and less in terms of days or hours, the past, or the future; they live only in the present moment. You can effectively touch the life of the person in your care with simple, brief *moments* of pleasure and happiness. Even after whatever you do is forgotten, the happy feeling generated in those moments can persist, potentially improving both their behavior and the ambiance in your home.

Caregivers can have a profound influence on the emotional state of people with Alzheimer's disease.

What are some things you can do to create more moments of happiness for the person in your care?

Are there things that create negative feelings for this person that can be avoided?

How would you now answer the two questions in the first paragraph?

My journal . . .

Day 43

Good?

*And we know that God causes everything to work
together for the good of those who love God and are
called according to his purpose for them.*

ROMANS 8:28

Julie wondered, "Does anything good ever come from
Alzheimer's disease?"

Many people would tell Julie that the answer is no.
They cite the heartbreak of watching a loved one decline
cognitively and physically. They point to the financial,
emotional, and physical burdens the disease places on
everyone it touches, especially family care partners.
There is nothing good about Alzheimer's disease, they
say, and nothing good comes from it.

Others, with equal sincerity, would tell Julie, "While
Alzheimer's is not good in itself, good *does* come out of
it." Some say that because of their loved one's disease,
they have grown closer to certain friends or family members,
or to God. Others say it has forced them to learn
new skills, such as managing money or cooking. Still

others recognize, with varying degrees of amazement, that while they have been faithfully caring for their loved one, good things have been quietly developing in a place they never expected—within themselves.

- Stan reflected, "Caregiving has helped me be more aware of others' needs and less selfish."

- Angie said, "I have become much stronger and more capable of handling things than I ever thought possible. I have found my voice—I am not afraid to speak up and advocate for my husband."

- Paul noted, "For many years, I followed a busy and structured schedule during the day. Caregiving has, out of necessity, made me more flexible and patient."

- Penny said, "This experience has taught me that love is an action verb, rather than a thought or a feeling."

In our book *Keeping Love Alive as Memories Fade*, my coauthor Ed Shaw reflected:

> *I have seen good come from this journey of Rebecca, my wife, with Alzheimer's disease. My daughters . . . and I are closer than ever. We have learned to hold one another up. We depend on one another. Other relationships have also been strengthened*

with family members, friends, and coworkers . . . The
Memory Counseling Program, now a program of
Wake Forest Baptist Health, did not exist five years
ago, and would not exist had Rebecca not developed
Alzheimer's disease. This counseling program has now
served hundreds of individuals, couples, and families
impacted by dementia through counseling sessions
and support groups.[1]

All of these dementia caregivers have discovered, perhaps somewhat to their surprise, that the truth of Romans
8:28 applies even to dementia and dementia caregiving.

Does anything good ever come from Alzheimer's disease?

REFLECTIONS ON *GOOD?*

What good has come from your caregiving experience
so far?

If you cannot yet point to anything good that has resulted from your loved one's dementia, circle the key words in Romans 8:28 and ask God to show you, in time, how this verse applies in your personal circumstances.

> "And we know that God causes everything to work together for the good of those who love God and are called according to his purpose for them." (Romans 8:28)

My journal . . .

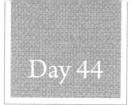

Spiritual Milk

Jesus answered, "It is written: 'Man shall not live by bread alone, but by every word that comes from the mouth of God.'"

MATTHEW 4:4 (ESV)

One of God's Old Testament names is *El Shaddai.* By itself, the Hebrew word *El* means God. *Shaddai* is thought to be derived from a word meaning "breast." When these words are combined, the name *El Shaddai* speaks of God's desire to nourish us and meet our needs, much as a loving mother would tenderly nurse her own infant.

In the New Testament, we see the spiritual-nourisher theme in the words of Peter. He tells believers, "Like newborn infants, long for the pure spiritual milk, that by it you may grow up into salvation . . . " (1 Peter 2:2 ESV). Peter wants Christ-followers to realize that as we saturate our minds and hearts with the Word of God, the Bible, this "spiritual milk" causes our spiritual growth.

True believers can either be spiritually well nourished or malnourished. It all depends on how often and how deeply we drink of the spiritual milk of the Word of God. Human beings require daily physical nourishment, whether they are newborn babies or senior adults. Without food and water, people of all ages will grow weak and sick. This is also true in the spiritual sense. This is exactly the point Jesus was making when He said, "It is written, 'Man shall not live by bread alone, but by every word that comes from the mouth of God'" (Matthew 4:4 ESV). Jesus spoke these words to Satan when he came to tempt Him after a forty-day fast. Satan may have thought he would have an advantage by tempting Christ when he was physically weak from fasting. But because Jesus' heart and mind were saturated with the Scriptures, He was spiritually strong. He spoke the Word from memory and did not yield to temptation.

Since we, like Jesus, are both physical and spiritual creatures, we too face both spiritual and physical battles. To be both physically and spiritually strong we require both physical and spiritual food each day. Most of us can count on one hand the times we have forgotten to eat a meal. Spiritual nourishment is just as vital as physical food, especially during the challenging season of life known as caregiving.

If you are feeling spiritually weak or are wavering in your faith right now, drink deeply from the pure, nourishing milk of the Word of God and be strengthened.

Let *El Shaddai* nourish you from His Word today and every day.

Drink deeply from the pure, nourishing milk of the Word of God and be strengthened.

REFLECTIONS ON *SPIRITUAL MILK*

On a scale of 1–10, if 1 is empty and 10 is full, how spiritually well nourished do you feel today?

What could you change that would allow you to consistently score a 10?

My journal . . .

The Loss of "Us"

The prayer of David, the shepherd/psalmist:

> *Turn to me and be gracious to me,*
> *for I am lonely and afflicted.*

PSALM 25:16 (ESV)

In *Keeping Love Alive as Memories Fade: The 5 Love Languages and the Alzheimer's Journey*, my coauthors and I highlighted the loneliness that often accompanies caregiving for a loved one with dementia. In the third chapter, we wrote: "Many care partners speak of the loneliness they experience as their loved one declines, leaving them more and more emotionally isolated."

One spouse caregiver, Marcus, described his lonely emotional isolation as "the loss of 'us.'" He said, "Gone is the ability to have 'couple secrets.' Gone is the intimacy of the 'us'—the private moments shared just by us, even in a crowd. This loss of the 'us' is the worst loss of all. This loss of couple intimacy, both physical and emotional, creates a void. It is impossible to describe this because we are both here, more connected than ever, but our roles are completely different, and my loneliness is too profound even for me to understand."

As Marcus discovered, when dementia renders a person unable to hold up their side of the relationship, the other person feels the disconnection acutely. While no one else can take the place of a husband or wife, mom or dad, it is very important to seek connection and fellowship with others who can provide spiritual and emotional support as the loved one's dementia progresses.

It is imperative that you, the caregiver, do not become isolated. We are created by God to be in relationship with others. We are not built for isolation; we're built for social connection. Often, the best support comes from others who have walked in our shoes and really understand what we are going through. Connecting with other dementia caregivers in a support group, even online, can help address the loneliness of caring for a cognitively declining person.

Psalm 68:6 says, "God places the lonely in families." If your loved one's dementia has left you feeling lonely, and if your biological family is perhaps not as supportive as you would like, ask God to help you create and connect with a "family" of fellow caregivers, Christian friends, and others.

It is imperative that you, the caregiver,
do not become isolated.

REFLECTIONS ON *THE LOSS OF "US"*

How did you feel as you read Marcus's description of "the loss of 'us'"?

What options can you pursue to increase your connections with others?

My journal . . .

When Colors Fade

*Jesus spoke to them again: "I am the light of the world.
Anyone who follows me will never walk in the darkness
but will have the light of life."*

JOHN 8:12 (CSB)

When my friend Eileen prays, both privately and aloud with others, she sometimes speaks to God using one of His many Old Testament names. Once, when I told her I had begun a new writing project, she offered to pray for me, saying she would be "calling upon Elohim to guide" me. She said this because writing is a creative endeavor, and God's "Creator" name is Elohim. This Hebrew name for God is used in Genesis 1:1, the first verse of the Bible: "In the beginning God (Elohim) created the heavens and the earth."

The opening chapter of Genesis also describes another of Elohim's amazing first creations: light. It mentions the sun, moon, and stars, citing the creation of physical light as the way to set day apart from night. After the book of Genesis, light is mentioned in many places throughout the Bible, but now physical light takes on additional meaning. In both the Old and New Testaments, light and darkness serve as a metaphor that helps us understand spiritual truths.

In the physical world, the color of an object comes from the way it reflects the light that falls on it. Under white light, colors are natural and vibrant. As filters are applied, objects reflect less and less light, making colors look darker. In the world of dementia caregiving, a similar thing can happen. Shelley, a discouraged caregiver, said she no longer has many opportunities for play or joy, as if the color has been drained out of her life. For Shelley, the daily strain of caring for her loved one has become like a filter that has cast a darkening shadow over the colors of her life.

Perhaps you can relate to Shelley. Does it seem that the stresses and duties of caregiving have conspired to squeeze the joy out of your days? Are the once-vibrant colors of your life now faded and dull? If your life seems steeped in bland hues of grey, it's time to step aside from your responsibilities long enough to recharge your spiritual batteries.

Ask a friend to spend time with your loved one so you can spend time in the presence of Elohim, the majestic Creator of light. Let your inner gaze fall as well upon Jesus, revealed in the New Testament as the Light of the World. Rest. Worship. Enjoy the sweet fellowship of your God. Bask in His brilliance until you can say with the psalmist, "The LORD, my God, lights up my darkness" (Psalm 18:28).

Rest. Worship. Enjoy the sweet fellowship of your God.

REFLECTIONS ON *WHEN COLORS FADE*

According to John 8:12, how can you be sure you will never walk in spiritual darkness?

How do the stresses and strains of caregiving "fade the colors of life"? How can you keep your "colors" from fading?

My journal . . .

Unintentional Sins

My protection and success come from God alone.
He is my refuge, a Rock where no enemy can reach me.

PSALM 62:7 (TLB)

Twelve years ago, Brian told his wife, Anna, "I will never touch you again." To Anna's heartbreak, it's a promise he has kept. Ironically, however, Brian imposes unwanted hugs upon strangers in the grocery store, unsuspecting male clerks in home-improvement stores, and the staff at his doctor's office. And while he won't touch Anna, on occasion he has approached women he did not know and made sexually suggestive comments. While these incidents cause Anna embarrassment and pain, she knows Brian acts this way because he has a type of dementia that causes extreme behavior and personality changes.

For many caregivers, the most challenging aspects of dementia are in the behavioral realm. It is important to remember, and to remind others, that the offensive or inappropriate behaviors of a person with dementia are not deliberate; they are caused by *brain damage*. When people with dementia step outside the lines, both social and biblical, it's wise to respond as Anna does, with grace and patience.

As with Brian, the brain damage of dementia explains many other inappropriate behaviors and "unintentional sins" of those with dementia. Some examples:

- People with dementia may shoplift, but not because they are trying to get something for nothing. They may not realize that they are in a store, or they may have forgotten that there is a need to pay.[1]

- When dementia has affected the frontal lobes of the brain, people may lose the ability to inhibit or restrain their speech. When a person becomes *dis*-inhibited they may say rude, insensitive, blunt, or insulting things to others. Because they have lost the ability to "filter" their speech, they speak impulsively without tact or love. They may say things to others such as, "You're really fat," or "I don't like you."

- People with dementia may complain—a lot—much to the chagrin of caregivers who may be making personal sacrifices in order to take care of their demented loved one. The complaints may actually have little to do with the caregiver. Because of memory loss and other brain changes, the person with dementia may be struggling to make sense of their world and feeling frustrated by their inability to communicate well. They may feel confused and unsettled, while also grieving their loss of independence. Complaints may just be the release valve for their many pent-up fears and feelings.

Do any of these scenarios sound familiar, dear caregiver?

As you seek to respond with grace to hurtful or embarrassing words and actions that occur due to brain damage, realizing they are not deliberate, you may nonetheless feel the sting of these offenses. To you, the gracious caregiver, God offers Himself as your constant, compassionate place of refuge.

The offensive or inappropriate behaviors of a person with dementia are not deliberate.

REFLECTIONS ON *UNINTENTIONAL SINS*

Does it help you to know that someone's offensive behaviors and comments are caused by the brain damage of dementia?

What is your response to the idea of unintentional sin?

Does the fact that an offense was not deliberate change its impact on you? On others?

My journal . . .

Day 48

Persist

When I am in distress, I call to you, because you answer me.
PSALM 86:7 (NIV)

Throughout the stories of the Bible, God's people affirmed again and again that God had listened to their prayers and answered them. Some examples:

ISAAC: "Isaac prayed to the LORD on behalf of his wife, because she was childless. The LORD answered his prayer, and his wife Rebekah became pregnant."[1]

JONAH: "In my great trouble I cried to the Lord and he answered me; from the depths of death I called, and Lord, you heard me!"[2]

DAVID: "... the LORD answered his prayer in behalf of the land, and the plague on Israel was stopped."[3]

HANNAH: "So in the course of time Hannah became pregnant and gave birth to a son. She named him Samuel, saying, 'Because I asked the LORD for him.'"[4]

JACOB: "For we are going to Bethel," he told them, "and I will build an altar there to the God who answered my prayers in the day of my distress, and was with me on my journey."[5]

Today, thousands upon thousands of Christ-followers can affirm from their own experience that God still hears and answers the prayers of His people. Sometimes our prayers are answered quickly; other times, we may wait for answers with no understanding about the reason for the delay. While we wait, Jesus, who fully understands the spiritual realm as well as God's plan for our lives, urges us to persist in prayer. He says, "And so I tell you, keep on asking, and you will receive what you ask for. Keep on seeking, and you will find. Keep on knocking, and the door will be opened to you. For everyone who asks, receives. Everyone who seeks, finds. And to everyone who knocks, the door will be opened."[6]

One of the great mysteries of persistent prayer is how it sometimes changes something other than our circumstances; sometimes it changes *us* by aligning our desires with the will of God. This was Paul's experience. He wrote,

> *So to keep me from becoming conceited because of the surpassing greatness of the revelations, a thorn was given me in the flesh, a messenger of Satan to*

harass me, to keep me from becoming conceited. Three times I pleaded with the Lord about this, that it should leave me. But he said to me, 'My grace is sufficient for you, for my power is made perfect in weakness.' Therefore I will boast all the more gladly of my weaknesses, so that the power of Christ may rest upon me. For the sake of Christ, then, I am content with weaknesses, insults, hardships, persecutions, and calamities. For when I am weak, then I am strong."[7]

The lesson to be learned from Paul is: pray about your every caregiving concern with the attitude, "Thy will be done." Persist in prayer until God either changes the circumstance or changes your desire in a way that aligns with His higher plan.

Pray about your every caregiving concern with the attitude, "Thy will be done."

REFLECTIONS ON *PERSIST*

When your prayers are not answered quickly, how do you respond?

What effect does persisting in prayer have upon believers?

My journal . . .

Do You Have a "Shadow"?

Very early in the morning, while it was still dark,
Jesus got up, left the house and went off to a
solitary place, where he prayed.

MARK 1:35 (NIV)

Everywhere He went, Jesus was constantly pressed in by crowds. He taught with such astonishing wisdom and authority that people gathered by the thousands to listen. Throngs of people followed after Him, hoping to witness a miracle or get close enough just to touch Him. People suffering from every imaginable disease or affliction pursued Him, seeking healing. On one such occasion, the whole town gathered at the door of the home where Jesus was staying with friends.[1] On another occasion, the crowd surrounding the house where He was teaching was so enormous that four men could not manage to get their paralyzed friend through the throng. Undaunted, they dug through the roof above the place where Jesus stood and lowered the man down through the opening on a mat.[2]

231

Day by day, Jesus fulfilled the purpose for which He had come to earth. Though His days were full, eternally significant, and joyous, like us, He also grew weary. Wisely, He sought times of solitude to restore and refresh himself physically, emotionally, and spiritually.

If you care for a person who "shadows" you, you are well acquainted with the frustration and weariness that come from rarely having time alone. In the latter part of Alzheimer's disease, people want to stay physically close to their primary caregiver. To them, the caregiver represents safety, security, and protection. The caregiver is their anchor in an increasingly incomprehensible world. A person with Alzheimer's disease may literally follow their caregiver around all day, just as a small child follows a parent, never letting that parent out of their sight.

Betsy's husband even follows her to the bathroom. "It's like being glued at the hip," she said, clearly exasperated at her loss of personal space. Betsy understands that "it's the disease, not the person." She also realizes that her husband shadows her because he feels fearful and insecure. Even though she understands these things and cares deeply for her husband, Betsy still feels violated by his continual shadowing.

While there is no totally satisfying remedy for shadowing, it can be helpful to pay more attention to each person's greatest need:

Their Need—The person shadowing you is fearful. You can help soothe their fears in two ways: (1) Strive to keep their environment calm, their daily routine predictable, and their activities uncomplicated. (2) Repeat reassuring verbal messages over and over, using the same words each time: "You are safe"; "I love you"; "Everything is okay."[3]

Your Need—Do you feel smothered by the continual shadowing of the person in your care? Are you are craving solitude? If so, there's no need to feel bad about it. It's normal to feel this way; many caregivers do. Remember, even Jesus needed time alone! Address your need by giving yourself the gift of solitude. If you can afford it, hire a respite caregiver. If money is in short supply, ask your family and friends to take turns providing respite care so you can recharge physically, emotionally, and spiritually, just as Jesus did.

Even Jesus needed time alone.

REFLECTIONS ON *DO YOU HAVE A "SHADOW"?*

Why did Jesus spend time alone when there were always so many people who needed His help?

How can you follow Jesus' example of emotional, spiritual, and physical self-care without feeling guilty or selfish?

My journal . . .

Anchored

We have this hope as an anchor for the soul, firm and secure.
HEBREWS 6:19A (csb)

Imagine a ship securely tethered to an anchor that rests deep below on the ocean floor. Though a storm is raging and the waves are fierce and violent, the ship's crew is remarkably calm. They know their anchor is unbreakable and immovable. No matter how angry the sea becomes, or how the ship may pitch and rock, the crew remains peaceful, knowing their safety is assured.

This calm in the midst of a stormy sea is a metaphor for the Christian life. Matthew Henry's Commentary offers a vivid description of the metaphor:

> *We are in this world as a ship at sea, liable to be tossed up and down, and in danger of being cast away. Our souls are the vessels. The comforts, expectations, graces, and happiness of our souls are the precious cargo with which these vessels are loaded. Heaven is the harbor to which we sail. The temptations, persecutions,*

and afflictions that we encounter, are the winds and waves that threaten our shipwreck. We have need of an anchor to keep us sure and steady, or we are in continual danger . . . [Christ] is the object, he is the anchor-hold of the believer's hope.[1]

Henry's commentary pairs two metaphors that have special significance: the anchor and the ocean. Since the early days of the Christian faith, the anchor has been a symbol of eternal security; Jesus Himself anchors us in heaven. As you can perhaps personally attest, the volatile ocean is not just an apt metaphor for life, but also for the caregiving journey. In everyday life, these metaphors often collide: the ocean (the stresses and trials of life) tugs relentlessly upon the anchor of faith. Yet, despite storms and crashing waves, the anchor holds secure. Christians, by their faith in Jesus, are unshakably moored "to the very throne of God."[2]

While few things in this life are certain, we can be sure that the storms of life will continue. As you navigate the unpredictable waters of the caregiving journey, the most important task before you is to check your moorings. Are you securely tethered to the "anchor-hold of the believer's hope"—Jesus Christ? He alone assures your safe passage not just through the storms of caregiving, but throughout all of life and eternity.

Faith in Jesus anchors us to the very throne of God.

REFLECTIONS ON *ANCHORED*

Jesus is the "anchor that assures your safe passage not just through the storms of caregiving, but through all of life and eternity." What does this mean?

Based on the verse below, how securely does Jesus anchor believers in eternity?

"I give them eternal life, and they will never perish. No one can snatch them away from me" (John 10:28).

Are you sure that you are anchored in heaven? If not, according to the verse below, how can you be sure?

For if you tell others with your own mouth that Jesus Christ is your Lord and believe in your own heart that God has raised him from the dead, you will be saved (Romans 10:9 TLB).

My journal . . .

God's Opportunity

"Neither this man nor his parents sinned,"
Jesus answered. "This came about so that God's
works might be displayed in him."

JOHN 9:3 (CSB)

People have always wondered whether illness or adversity means that the affected person is reaping a penalty for some sin. Jesus made it clear to His disciples that this is definitely not always the case. One day while they were out walking, they passed by a man who had been blind from birth. The disciples wanted to know whose sin had caused the problem: was it the man's own sin or was it the sin of his parents? Jesus told them that it was neither. The man was born blind, He said, so that God's power could be demonstrated in his life.

Jesus went on to show them exactly what He meant. He spat on the ground to make mud and then spread the mud on the blind man's eyes. He told the man to go wash the mud off in the Pool of Siloam. He did so and came back seeing![1] God was greatly glorified by this miracle.

Down through the ages, this story in the gospel of John has revealed to millions that the man's blindness was not the result of sin, but was actually planned by God for a good and God-glorifying purpose.

People today think in much the same way as people did in Bible times. Dementia caregivers sometimes wonder if they, the caregiver, could have done something to cause their family member's dementia, and as a result, have put themselves in the caregiving role. Responding to that notion, one care partner said, "We could look at it as we're being punished—or we could turn it around." Turning it around means thinking of it as a God-given opportunity, he said, "to show unselfish love." He told his caregiver support group, "I think that's what we all do."

A wise individual in a bygone era once said, "Every difficulty that presents itself to us, if we receive it in the right way, is God's opportunity."[2] These true, timeless words describe the mindset of many Christian caregivers today. Even though they would never have chosen the dementia journey for their loved one or for themselves as caregivers, they are resolute in their belief that when it is fully surrendered to God, even dementia becomes "God's opportunity."

Every difficulty, if received in the right way,
becomes God's opportunity.

REFLECTIONS ON *GOD'S OPPORTUNITY*

How do you feel about the idea that, when fully surrendered to God, even dementia becomes "God's opportunity"?

How does your loved one's dementia create opportunities for you "to show unselfish love"?

My journal . . .

Tears

*You keep track of all my sorrows. You have collected all my
tears in your bottle. You have recorded each one in your book.*

PSALM 56:8

Walking with a loved one on their dementia journey can be heartbreaking, and caregivers shed
many tears along the way. If you are a dementia caregiver
yourself, you will no doubt relate to Gracie and Dawn,
who both graciously agreed to answer my question, *"In
your role as a caregiver, what makes you cry?"*

For Gracie, tears well up at the thought that she is
"married but single." She cries because caregiving is a
lonely task, made worse, she says, by disappointment
in family and friends who find ways of "excusing themselves from the journey." She cries when she thinks
about "what has been lost" and the fact that "today is the
best it will ever be." Her greatest heartbreak, she says, is
knowing that her husband "will never be my partner or
caregiver and cannot see that I am his."

Dawn said, "I shed tears for a long time when I could

no longer take care of my husband. Every day when I left him at the facility it was so sad to tell him he couldn't come home with me, then to come home by myself to an empty house." She has wept because "In the past I did not recognize that some of his unacceptable behavior was because of Alzheimer's, and he could not help it." Now her tears are for the future because "he is not able to have the relationship with his grandchildren that he would normally have loved." Even in the midst of her sadness, Dawn also feels "joy that one day this will be over and my husband will be with Jesus."

For caregivers like Gracie and Dawn, there is great comfort in John 11:35. Though it consists of just two words, this verse is powerful; it simply says, "Jesus wept." Those two brief words tell us that our Lord felt deep emotion just as caregivers do, and that He was not ashamed to shed tears as he stood with his friends Mary and Martha at the tomb of their brother, Lazarus, who was also His dear friend. In Hebrews we read this amazing verse: "While Jesus was here on earth, he offered prayers and pleadings, with a loud cry and tears, to the one who could rescue him from death. And God heard his prayers because of his deep reverence to God" (Hebrews 5:7). Thus, while in human form, even Jesus was not spared the sting and anguish of sin that are so familiar to all of us.

The Bible promises that one day "the Lord God will wipe away tears from all faces . . ." Until that wonderful day arrives, since the sins and sorrows of this world moved our Lord to weep unashamedly, there is no reason for you to be ashamed of your tears either. Sometimes in the course of caring for a loved one with dementia, only tears can fully release the emotions that build up inside. Tears are a natural, God-designed way to relieve the grief, stress, and sadness that are sometimes part of the caregiver's journey.

> *Sometimes only tears can fully release the emotions that build up inside.*

REFLECTIONS ON *TEARS*

How are you impacted by the fact that Jesus felt deep emotion that moved Him to tears?

What emotions do you experience as you care for your loved one that trigger your tears?

How does Psalm 56:8 assure you that God is personally aware of your deepest feelings?

My journal . . .

_____

_____

_____

_____

_____

_____

_____

_____

The Spirit Prays for You

*We do not know what we ought to pray for, but the
Spirit himself intercedes for us through wordless groans.
And he who searches our hearts knows the mind
of the Spirit, because the Spirit intercedes for God's people
in accordance with the will of God.*

ROMANS 8:26–27 (NIV)

When caring for a person with dementia, sometimes it's hard to pray. The heart may be so full of emotion or grief, and the body so fatigued, that one can hardly find the words (or the energy) to pour it all out to God in prayer. You never need to fret or feel guilty about this; God understands more fully than you can humanly imagine.

When we, God's children, are so tired or discouraged or overwhelmed that we cannot pray, or when we simply can't find the right words to adequately express our needs to God, we can remind ourselves of the amazing truth that the Spirit Himself prays for us. The Holy Spirit knows our every thought and circumstance, and because

He also knows the will of the Father, He intercedes for us willingly, compassionately, and perfectly.

When prayerful words won't come, or when they fail to express what is in your heart, know that your concerns still reach the Father. The Holy Spirit takes even your poorest prayers and reframes them in His holy wisdom as He speaks of you before the heavenly throne. A. B. Simpson (1843–1919), founder of the Christian and Missionary Alliance, once said that

> *sometimes we do not understand any more than that God is praying for us, for something that needs His touch and that He understands. And so we can just pour out the fullness of our heart, the burden of our spirit, the sorrow that crushes us, and know that He hears, He loves, He understands, He receives; and He separates from our prayer all that is imperfect, ignorant and wrong, and presents the rest, with the incense of the great High Priest, before the throne on high; and our prayer is heard, accepted and answered in His name.*[1]

When prayerful words won't come, or when they fail to express what is in your heart, know that the Holy Spirit intercedes for you willingly, compassionately, and perfectly.

REFLECTIONS ON *THE SPIRIT PRAYS FOR YOU*

How does it make you feel to know that the Holy Spirit prays for you?

According to Romans 8:26–27, how does the Holy Spirit know what to pray for you?

My journal . . .

Hesed: God's Faithful Love

He has shown you, O mortal, what is good. And what does
the LORD require of you? To act justly and to love mercy
[hesed] and to walk humbly with your God.

MICAH 6:8 (NIV)

In contemporary American culture, *love* can mean many
things. We love everything from ice cream, comfy
jeans, and football teams to the new carpet at church. We
love our families and friends, our country, and maybe
country music as well. But none of that "love" comes
close to the truest, most perfect kind of love, which is the
love of God. There isn't even an English word that adequately captures the essence of this kind of love. There
is a Hebrew word, however, that does. That word is *hesed*
(HEH-sed).

Hesed has no exact English equivalent, so it has been
translated in many ways: loving-kindness, steadfast love,
loyalty, faithfulness, mercy, and covenant love. It may be
best described as a blend of love and loyalty. *Hesed* isn't

about romance. It is richer and deeper than that. It is love that intervenes on behalf of the one loved. It is not a feeling; it's an action. It is choice-driven, faithful love that can be counted on.

Hesed occurs numerous times in the Bible, in some of the most well-loved and oft-quoted verses. Some verses speak about God's *hesed* toward people; others speak of one person's expression of *hesed* to another. If *hesed* were substituted for the English word in Hosea 6:6, it would read, "For I desire *hesed*, not sacrifice, and acknowledgment of God rather than burnt offerings."[1] Lamentations 3:22 would say, "The *hesed* of the LORD never ends! His mercies never cease."[2] David's words to Mephibosheth would be, "I will surely show you *hesed* for the sake of your father Jonathan."[3] And Naomi's benediction to her daughters-in-law would be, "May the LORD show you *hesed*, as you have shown *hesed* to your dead husbands and to me."[4] In the New Testament story of the Good Samaritan, the word for mercy is translated *hesed* in the Greek Old Testament.[5]

Hesed is an above-and-beyond kind of love. In our book *Keeping Love Alive as Memories Fade*, this *hesed* love is a recurring theme. My coauthors and I chose this word to describe the "gold standard" of dementia care—the loyal, merciful, intentional love that intervenes on behalf of loved ones and comes to their rescue. This is the word that best describes the loyal love of so many caregivers whose family member can no longer love them back. Sadly, studies suggest that about half of all people with dementia are mistreated in some way. In stark, beautiful contrast to this, the *hesed* of Christian caregivers expresses the compassion, kindness, and mercy of God to those afflicted with dementia.

Loving another person is always a choice. If you provide care for someone with dementia, love is not always an easy choice. Ask God to help you continually choose to express *hesed* toward the person in your care.

Hesed is a love that intervenes on behalf of the one loved.

REFLECTIONS ON *HESED: GOD'S FAITHFUL LOVE*

List some of the ways God has expressed *hesed* toward you.

How might your expressions of *hesed* toward the person in your care display God's love for others to see?

My journal . . .

Day 55

Yes and No

Surely you desire integrity in the inner self,
and you teach me wisdom deep within.

PSALM 51:6 (CSB)

Many years ago, I learned something at a writers conference that became a guiding principle for my life. The seminar teacher told our group of aspiring writers that if we wanted to be successful at our craft, we would have to "narrow the channel to strengthen the stream." As the meaning of this rather cryptic advice dawned on me, I realized that the teacher had given us a memorable metaphor about priorities.

Just as water flows more powerfully through a narrow channel than through a broad one, writers must direct their time and energy into the "narrow channel" of writing instead of spreading them thinly across multiple pursuits that would siphon time away from writing. In other words, in order to fully say yes to writing, writers often have to say no to other things. Good things. Interesting and enjoyable things. Because there are only so many hours in a day and in a life, and in those finite hours we must choose wisely how we will expend our limited supply of mental and physical energy.

I now apply this principle to life in general: by saying *no* to lesser things, I can respond with a more enthusiastic *yes* to things that matter more to me. In caregiving, the words *yes* and *no* are of extraordinary importance for similar reasons. You have a limited supply of physical and emotional energy, and you have financial limits too. If you say yes when you know you should say no, or you say, "no thanks" to offers of help you need, you have not been truthful, and this is to your detriment.

If you tend to say *yes* when you really need to say *no*, or vice versa, it may be time to adopt Ephesians 4:15 as a guideline: "... we will lovingly follow the truth at all times—speaking truly, dealing truly, living truly... (TLB).

How does that work in practical terms? It means answering truthfully when you are asked:

- "Would you like to host the family for Christmas dinner this year?"
- "Is there anything you need right now?"
- "Can you loan me $500?"
- "Can I pick up something for you at the grocery store?"
- "I have a few hours free on Tuesday. Would you like a break?"

In the past, you may have declined help out of pride, or said yes when it was not in your best interests in order to please others. Now that you're a dementia caregiver, there's really no room for people pleasing. Give yourself permission to say no to activities that are draining or things you can't afford. Remind yourself that if you need help, it's definitely okay to accept help. In the "let's get real" world of caregiving, let truth reign!

Now that you're a dementia caregiver, there's really no room for people pleasing.

REFLECTIONS ON *YES AND NO*

If you tend to say yes when you should say no, or vice versa, why do you think this is so?

If you have trouble accepting help you truly need, why do you think this is so?

How can you apply Psalm 51:6 and Ephesians 4:15 in your life?

My journal . . .

Day 56

Temptation

Honor your marriage and its vows, and be pure; for God will surely punish all those who are immoral or commit adultery.

HEBREWS 13:4 (TLB)

Sex is a gift from God. He designed sex not only for pleasure and procreation, but also to bond a husband and wife to one another physically, emotionally, and spiritually. The sexual union makes two individuals into "one flesh."[1] In Christian marriage, Paul taught that couples have both the privilege and the duty of consistently meeting each other's sexual needs: "Do not deprive each other of sexual relations, unless you both agree to refrain from sexual intimacy for a limited time so you can give yourselves more completely to prayer. Afterward, you should come together again so that Satan won't be able to tempt you because of your lack of self-control" (1 Corinthians 7:5).

As this verse warns, a lack of sexual activity in marriage can make one vulnerable to temptation. This is an important issue for spouse caregivers because, almost always, dementia eventually brings sexual intimacy in marriage to an end. When couples know this ahead of time, they can make the most of their opportunities for intimacy now, and the care partner can prepare emotionally and spiritually for the time when sexual activity with their husband or wife will no longer be possible.

The loss of sexual intimacy in marriage challenges the moral and spiritual convictions of spouse care partners. If temptation comes, will they abandon their marriage vows? Will they dismiss God's command, "Do not commit adultery"[2]? Compare Robert's decision to the choice Dan made.

As her Alzheimer's disease progressed, Robert's wife, Mary, became hypersensitive to physical touch, which made her uncomfortable with sexual activity. In addition, as her memory faded, Mary literally forgot how to make love with Robert. Eventually, she reached the point where she no longer even recognized Robert as her spouse. After Mary forgot who he was, Robert felt he should no longer pursue any sexual activity with Mary. Though he and Mary no longer had a sexual relationship, Robert chose to keep his marriage vows. He remained celibate and avoided potentially adulterous relationships.

Dementia affected Dan's wife, Alicia, very differently than it affected Mary. Two years after her Alzheimer's diagnosis, Alicia became intensely and uncharacteristically interested in sex. She wanted to have sex with Dan every day. While Dan would have welcomed this in the earlier years of their marriage, it was a problem for him now. He felt that Alicia had been so changed by dementia that she was no longer the same person. He was so "turned off" by these changes in his wife that he no longer felt the least bit attracted to her. Even so, he wanted to be loyal to Alicia and was willing to continue a platonic "hugs and kisses only" relationship with her. After a while this became too difficult, and Dan was unable to avoid temptation. To meet his own sexual needs, Dan had affairs with several women even while continuing to provide care for Alicia.

If the day should arrive when sexual intimacy can no longer be a part of your marriage, how will you respond? Experts say it is easier to do the right thing in a tough moment if the decision has already been made ahead of time. So, decide now, ahead of time: will you choose Robert's path or Dan's?

The loss of sexual intimacy in marriage challenges the moral and spiritual convictions of spouse care partners.

REFLECTIONS ON *TEMPTATION*

How can making decisions ahead of time help you respond to temptation?

Why do you think Dan did not "take the high road"?

If you were Robert, how would you explain your decision to Dan?

My journal . . .

One

"The King will reply, 'Truly I tell you, whatever you did for one of the least of these brothers and sisters of mine, you did for me.'"

MATTHEW 25:40 (NIV)

Although Jesus came to die for the sins of the entire world, He is intensely concerned for the spiritual condition of each individual, each *one*. Luke chapter 15 contains a parable that reveals His focus on each of us, personally. He said, "What man among you, who has a hundred sheep and loses **one** of them, does not leave the ninety-nine in the open field and go after the lost **one** until he finds it? When he has found it, he joyfully puts it on his shoulders, and coming home, he calls his friends and neighbors together, saying to them, 'Rejoice with me, because I have found my lost sheep!' I tell you, in the same way, there will be more joy in heaven over **one** sinner who repents than over ninety-nine righteous people who don't need repentance."[1]

This same concern for individuals is revealed in

Jesus' conversations with Nicodemus the Pharisee,[2] with the Samaritan woman at the well,[3] and with Zacchaeus, the tax collector perched in the sycamore tree.[4] Even in the last hours of His earthly life, Jesus' concern was for individuals. While on the cross, He committed the care of His mother, Mary, to His beloved disciple, John,[5] and assured the repentant thief on the cross next to Him that "today you will be with me in paradise."[6]

Jesus also cares deeply for the *one* with physical needs. During His time on earth, though He healed so many, each of those 'many' was one precious, unique individual: Peter's mother-in-law, the centurion's daughter, and the paralyzed man, to name a few.[7]

Christ's concern has always been not only for the *one* but for the *whole* one: each individual's body, mind, and spirit. In Matthew 25, He speaks about a whole range of human needs: hunger and thirst, nakedness, loneliness, sickness, and the need for compassion and acceptance. Jesus so identifies with humanity that He plainly says that when we meet these needs for those He calls sisters and brothers it is the same as if we are doing it for Him. In saying this, He conferred upon care partners, including you, a holy privilege. All that you do for the *one* in your care, you do for Jesus.

All that you do for the one in your care, you do for Jesus.

REFLECTIONS ON *ONE*

In years past, what kind of relationship did you have with the *one* for whom you now provide care?

Does your history with this person make it easier or harder to treat this *one* as if he or she were Jesus?

How does Matthew 25:40 impact your attitude toward the *one* in your care?

My journal...

Silver Lining

*No discipline seems pleasant at the time, but painful.
Later on, however, it produces a harvest of righteousness and
peace for those who have been trained by it.*

HEBREWS 12:11 (NIV)

New believers sometimes expect that their faith in Christ will insulate them from problems and pain. The truth is that it does not. In fact, all of God's children go through hard times. None of us enjoy adversity, and all of us struggle to understand our suffering. Often, when facing a difficult situation, a Christian will say, "God allowed this to happen." The Bible makes it clear that God does not just *allow* our hard times; He personally brings them about. Consider these verses:

- "Is it not from the mouth of the Most High that both calamities and good things come?" (Lamentations 3:38 NIV).

- "I form the light and create darkness, I bring prosperity and create disaster; I, the LORD, do all these things" (Isaiah 45:7 NIV).

What perplexing verses! We know that we are dearly loved by God. *Why would He cause us to suffer?*

This mystery deepens when we read, "Though he brings grief, he will show compassion, so great is his unfailing love. For he does not willingly bring affliction or grief to anyone" (Lamentations 3:32–33 NIV). In this most poignant verse, we gain surprising insights about suffering. Not only does this verse affirm that, yes, God is the one who "brings grief," it also reveals that God's motive is love and that He does not *willingly* cause us to suffer. In other words, whenever God causes suffering, He remains loving, kind, and merciful toward us. He is moved to compassion by our pains. He takes no pleasure in our hard times and does not willingly put roadblocks in our path. As the New Living Translation of Lamentations 3:33 phrases it, God "does not enjoy hurting people or causing them sorrow." This brings us back to the same perplexing question: if God does not afflict us willingly, and takes no pleasure in doing so, and is even moved with compassion toward us when we are hurting . . . *why does He cause us to go through hard times?*

C. S. Lewis pondered this question and concluded that God allows us to experience low points in life to teach us lessons that we couldn't learn in any other way.[1] It is God's perfect love for us that compels Him to correct us, teach us, and increase our faith through hard times.

While there is no totally sufficient explanation for human suffering, the mystery is at least partly resolved for Christians by this pearl of truth: God places us in the hard circumstances that He knows are *necessary* to fulfill His good plan for our lives.

Be assured that the difficulties you experience on the caregiving journey are not random or meaningless. Hebrews 12:11 tells us that if we allow adversity to accomplish the purpose for which God sent it, "afterwards we can see the result, a quiet growth in grace and character" (TLB). This is the silver lining in the rain cloud of suffering.

God places us in the hard circumstances that He knows are necessary to fulfill His good plan for our lives.

REFLECTIONS ON *SILVER LINING*

How do you feel about the idea that God uses the hard times of life to teach us lessons that we could learn in no other way?

What does Lamentations 3:32–33 tell you about God's love for you?

My journal . . .

Day 59

Worry

*Give all your worries and cares to God,
for he cares about you.*

1 PETER 5:7

Gina has been the primary care partner for her husband since his diagnosis of Alzheimer's disease more than seven years ago. As his cognitive function continues to decline, Gina admits, "I spend hours worrying and afraid. Will we have enough money to care for him? Will I make the right decisions? Why didn't I think about these things sooner so we could plan together?"

Many dementia care partners like Gina are preoccupied with worry; some are overwhelmed by it. Common worries relate to:

- WANDERING ("What if the person with dementia wanders away and gets lost?")
- DRIVING ("How will the person with dementia react when it is time to take away the car keys? In the meantime, what if she causes a traffic accident?")

- **MONEY** ("How are we going to meet all the expenses that lie ahead? What if the person with dementia outlives their resources?")
- **CARE PARTNER HEALTH** ("What if I get sick or injured and can't take care of the person with dementia?")

Of course, worry is not unique to dementia care partners. All around the world, in every walk of life, people worry. Through the ages, philosophers have opined with nuggets of truth about worry:

> "Worry is like a rocking chair: it gives you something to do but never gets you anywhere."—*Erma Bombeck*

> "Worry often gives a small thing a big shadow."
> —*Swedish proverb*

> "Worry never robs tomorrow of its sorrow, it only saps today of its joy."—*Leo Buscaglia*

Every dementia care partner encounters difficult problems and faces tough decisions. However, some care partners meet these challenges head-on, energized by concern, while others are paralyzed by worry. Worry is debilitating because it is *problem*-focused; concern is empowering because it is *solution*-focused. For believers, worry reveals the depth of our trust in God. Pastor

Tim Keller has said, "Worry is not believing God will get it right . . ."[1]

Moving from the paralysis of worry to empowered concern can start by heeding Peter's counsel to the Jewish believers of Asia Minor: "Give all your worries and cares to God, for he cares about you."

Worry is not believing that God will get it right.

REFLECTIONS ON *WORRY*

If you are a worried care partner, take this step of faith:

1. In the first column below, list the things that worry you.

2. In the second column, list an action step for each worry, such as "call DMV about a driving evaluation for John."

3. In the third column, place a check mark as you commit each specific worry to God, one by one, according to 1 Peter 5:7, trusting that He will guide you as you take your action steps.

MY WORRIES	ACTION STEPS	COMMITTED TO GOD ✓

My journal...

_____

_____

_____

_____

_____

_____

Author and Finisher

*. . . let us run with endurance the race that is set
before us, looking unto Jesus, the author and finisher
of our faith, who for the joy that was set before Him
endured the cross, despising the shame, and has sat
down at the right hand of the throne of God.*

HEBREWS 12:1b–2 (NKJV)

Throughout the Bible, Jesus is described in at least
fifty different ways. Each of His titles or names is
like a facet of a diamond, revealing some unique aspect
of His glorious character. His many names include Lion
of Judah, Chief Cornerstone, Bridegroom, Good Shepherd, Messiah, King of Kings, True Vine, and Prince of
Peace. In one place, He is revealed as the "author and
finisher" of our faith—*your* faith. He is the Author; your
life is His manuscript. He's writing the eternal story of
your faith, your faithful caregiving, and your future here
on earth and in heaven.

A diagnosis of Alzheimer's disease has a way of
quickly putting earthly things into perspective. What-

ever seemed important only yesterday pales rapidly in the scorching light of a loved one's Alzheimer's diagnosis. My friend Ed Shaw, whose career as a radiation oncologist earned him worldwide recognition, reordered his priorities almost overnight when his fifty-three-year-old wife was diagnosed with early-onset Alzheimer's disease. He recalls, "All of a sudden, my goal of being the best brain tumor radiation oncologist in the world didn't seem so important. But my wedding vows did: *for richer or poorer, in sickness and in health, 'til death do you part.* My goal became helping Rebecca live each day to its fullest. I wanted to cross the finish line with her, when death would part us."

As the Finisher of faith, Jesus completes what He starts. He crossed the finish line in His earthly race to secure our salvation for eternity. As our faithful Lord, He does not merely watch our races from the sidelines; He runs alongside us, every step of the way, enabling us to also complete what we start. With His help, after nine years of faithful caregiving, Ed crossed the finish line with his beloved Rebecca. Your Lord, the Author and Finisher of your faith, will enable you to do the same.

Run with endurance the race set before you and keep your eyes on Jesus!

He is the Author; your life is His manuscript.

REFLECTIONS ON *AUTHOR AND FINISHER*

Ponder Hebrews 12:1b–2. What comes to mind as you picture Jesus, the author and finisher of your faith, walking with you into the future?

My journal . . .

Postscript

As I was writing this devotional, a question kept coming to my mind. If you provide care for a person with dementia who has never professed faith in Christ, perhaps you have this same question. My thinking went something like this: in the early stages of dementia, when people can still carry on conversations and make decisions, it is reasonable to assume that an unsaved person can respond to the gospel. But, I wondered, as the disease progresses on into the middle and late stages, could salvation still occur?

I decided to ask Dr. Ed Shaw and Dr. Gary Chapman for their thoughts. These two gentlemen were my coauthors for the book *Keeping Love Alive as Memories Fade: The 5 Love Languages and the Alzheimer's Journey.* Ed Shaw, a physician and mental health counselor, was the primary caregiver for nearly a decade for his wife who had Alzheimer's disease. Gary Chapman is my pastor and the author of *The 5 Love Languages* and numerous other books.

The question I asked them was: *Do you think that an unsaved person in the middle or late stage of Alzheimer's can respond to the gospel?*

I would like to share their responses with you.

> Ed said, "What an interesting question. My opinion is yes, an unsaved person with Alzheimer's can respond to the gospel, but it may happen in a supernatural way that is between that person and the Holy Spirit. For the Christian caregiver worried about their spouse, I would convey this in a way that gives hope regarding their unsaved loved one."

> Gary said, "Honestly, I don't know. I do know that God knows the human heart and has His own way of communicating to us individually. So, what Ed said is certainly possible. I've always found Deuteronomy 29:29 helpful: 'The secret things belong to the Lord our God.'"

Their responses affirmed what I too had suspected. While there is no way to be sure that a person in mid or late dementia can respond to the gospel, we can be certain of two things: spiritual rebirth is God's own mysterious work, and no challenge, not even dementia, is too hard for Him.

So, can we ask the Holy Spirit to work in the lives of unbelievers with advanced dementia? Yes, we can. Can we speak to them about salvation as our kindnesses also speak to them of God's love? We certainly can.

We can do these things, despite our uncertainties, because we are entrusting them to a loving God who knows all hearts.

The secret things belong to the Lord our God.

Alphabetical Listing of Titles and Key Verses

Notes

Day 1: The Words of God
1. Hebrews 13:8.

Day 2: The Unexpected Journey
1. Mrs. Charles E. Cowman (compiler), "October 31," *Streams in the Desert* (Grand Rapids: Zondervan, 1982), 118.
2. James 2:23.
3. Proverbs 18:24 ESV.

Day 3: Caregiver School
1. "How do I deal with the stress, frustration and anger associated with caregiving?" https://www.caring.com/questions/stress-and-anger-from-caregiving. Last updated Nov 10, 2016.

Day 4: Why?
1. Elta M. Lewis (lyrics) and William James Kirkpatrick (music), "Whate'er It Be (I take my portion from Thy hand)," 1893.

Day 5: Stay Where You Are
1. Addie Zierman, "If You Feel Far Away From God, Guess Who Moved?," *Addie Zierman* (blog), http://addiezierman.com/2014/06/16/if-you-feel-far-away-from-god-at-deeper-story/.
2. John 15:4 ESV.
3. John 15:9 ESV.

Day 12: The Power of Music
1. Zephaniah 3:17 ESV.
2. Psalm 135:3.
3. Revelation 5:13.

Day 13: Feeling Guilty
1. Deborah Barr, Edward G. Shaw, and Gary Chapman, *Keeping Love Alive as Memories Fade: The 5 Love Languages and the Alzheimer's Journey* (Chicago: Northfield Publishing, 2016), 151.
2. David Ferguson, "God's Freedom from False Guilt," http://www.preachitteachit.org/articles/detail/gods-freedom-from-false-guilt/.

Day 14: Gratitude

1. "The Road to Resilience," *American Psychological Association*, http://www.apa.org/helpcenter/road-resilience.aspx.
2. Ibid.

Day 17: Everything to God in Prayer

1. Lindsay Terry, "What a Friend We Have in Jesus," http://staugustine.com/living/religion/2015-04-23/story-behind-song-what-friend-we-have-jesus.
2. "What a Friend We Have in Jesus," lyrics. http://library.timelesstruths.org/music/What_a_Friend_We_Have_in_Jesus/ (copyright status: public domain).
3. "What a Friend We Have in Jesus." http://www.josephscriven.org/Home/Home.html.

Day 18: Bad Day

1. John 16:33 NIV.
2. Matthew 6:34 CSB.
3. Lamentations 3:22–23.

Day 20: Bugs and Oil

1. W. Phillip Keller, *A Shepherd Looks at Psalm 23* (Grand Rapids: Zondervan, 2007), 138–42.

Day 22: Love Languages

1. Deborah Barr, Edward G. Shaw, and Gary Chapman, *Keeping Love Alive as Memories Fade: The 5 Love Languages and the Alzheimer's Journey* (Chicago: Northfield Publishing, 2016). Used by permission.

Day 24: Life: It's So Daily

1. Exodus 16:4 NIV.
2. Matthew 6:11 ESV.
3. Hebrews 3:13 CSB.
4. 2 Corinthians 11:28.

Day 25: Laughter

1. Nicole Savini, "What's So Funny? Caregiving with a Smile," *The Association for Frontotemporal Degeneration*, http://www.theaftd.org/front-page/comedy-centrals-nicole-savini-asks-whats-so-funny.
2. Deborah Barr, Edward G. Shaw, and Gary Chapman, *Keeping Love Alive as Memories Fade: The 5 Love Languages and the Alzheimer's Journey* (Chicago: Northfield Publishing, 2016), 191.

3. Lawrence Robinson, Melinda Smith, MA, and Jeanne Segal, PhD. "Laughter Is the Best Medicine: The Health Benefits of Humor and Laughter." https://www.helpguide.org/articles/emotional-health/laughter-is-the-best-medicine.htm. Updated January 2017.

4. Sherri Snelling, "Why Laughter Is Crucial for Care partners," http://www.nextavenue.org/why-laughter-crucial-care partners/.

5. Markham Heid, "You Asked: Does Laughing Have Real Health Benefits?", *Time*, http://time.com/3592134/laughing-health-benefits/.

Day 26: Paraclete (The Helper Jesus Sent)

1. John 14:16; John 14:26; John 15:26; John 16:7.

2. "*parakletos*," Strong's 3875.

3. J. Brown, *The Paraclete*, sermon, http://biblehub.com/sermons/auth/brown/the_paraclete.htm.

Day 27: Christ-Following

1. Behind the Song with Kevin Davis, #118 "More Like Falling in Love" by Jason Gray. http://www.newreleasetoday.com/article.php?article_id=370.

Day 28: Weary?

1. "A Good Night's Sleep," *National Institute on Aging*, https://www.nia.nih.gov/health/publication/good-nights-sleep#aging.

Day 29: Contentment: Paul's Secret

1. John Darby's Synopsis of the New Testament, commentary for Philippians 4, Bible Study Tools, https://www.biblestudytools.com/commentaries/john-darbys-synopsis-of-the-new-testament/philippians/philippians-4.html.

2. "St. Paul." YourDictionary, n.d., http://biography.yourdictionary.com/st-paul.

3. Philippians 3:4–6.

4. 2 Corinthians 11:24–26.

Day 30: God's Masterpiece

1. Henry and Richard Blackaby and Claude King, *Experiencing God: Knowing and Doing the Will of God,* revised and expanded edition (Nashville: B&H Books, 2008), 121.

2. Deborah Barr, Edward G. Shaw, and Gary Chapman, *Keeping Love Alive as Memories Fade: The 5 Love Languages and the Alzheimer's Journey* (Chicago: Northfield Publishing, 2016), 159–60.

3. Ibid., 195.

Day 33: Pruning
1. Galatians 5:22–23.
2. Matthew 6:34.
3. Philippians 4:13 ESV.

Day 34: Faithfulness
1. Deborah Barr, Edward G. Shaw, and Gary Chapman, *Keeping Love Alive as Memories Fade: The 5 Love Languages and the Alzheimer's Journey* (Chicago: Northfield Publishing, 2016), 67.
2. Ibid., 194–95.

Day 35: In Their Shoes
1. Deborah Barr, Edward G. Shaw, and Gary Chapman, *Keeping Love Alive as Memories Fade: The 5 Love Languages and the Alzheimer's Journey* (Chicago: Northfield Publishing, 2016), 188–89.
2. "Sympathy vs. Empathy," *Everything After Z* (blog), http://www.dictionary.com/e/empathy-vs-sympathy/.
3. Guy Winch, PhD, "How to Test Your Empathy," https://www.psychologytoday.com/blog/the-squeaky-wheel/201103/how-test-your-empathy.
4. David F. Swink, "I Don't Feel Your Pain: Overcoming Roadblocks to Empathy," *Psychology Today*, March 7, 2013, https://www.psychologytoday.com/blog/threat-management/201303/i-dont-feel-your-pain-overcoming-roadblocks-empathy.

Day 36: Shalom
1. Isaiah 9:6.
2. Colossians 1:20 TLB.

Day 38: In the Potter's Hands
1. Dan Graves, "Sarah Pollard Didn't Like Her Name," http://www.christianity.com/church/church-history/timeline/1801-1900/sarah-pollard-didnt-like-her-name-11630530.html.
2. "Have Thine Own Way, Lord," https://en.wikipedia.org/wiki/Have_Thine_Own_Way,_Lord.

Day 40: Live in Peace
1. George Kraus, *Helping the Alzheimer's Patient: Plain Talk and Practical Tools* (DVD), presented through PESI, copyright 2011, MEDS PDN, Eau Claire, WI,10.
2. Ibid., 10.

Day 42: Feelings and Moments

1. Edmarie Guzma et al., "Feelings Without Memory in Alzheimer Disease," *Cognitive and Behavioral Neurology* 27, no. 3 (2014): 117–29.
2. John Riehl, "Alzheimer's patients can still feel the emotion long after the memories have vanished," *IowaNow*, September 24, 2014, https://now.uiowa.edu/2014/09/alzheimers-patients-can-still-feel-emotion-long-after-memories-have-vanished.

Day 43: Good?

1. Deborah Barr, Edward G. Shaw, and Gary Chapman, *Keeping Love Alive as Memories Fade: The 5 Love Languages and the Alzheimer's Journey* (Chicago: Northfield Publishing, 2016), 201.

Day 47: Unintentional Sins

1. Nancy L. Mace and Peter V. Rabins, *The 36-Hour Day: A Family Guide for People Who Have Alzheimer's Disease, Related Dementias, and Memory Loss* (Baltimore: Johns Hopkins University Press, 2011), 258.

Day 48: Persist

1. Genesis 25:21 NIV.
2. Jonah 2:2 TLB.
3. 2 Samuel 24:25 NIV.
4. 1 Samuel 1:20 NIV.
5. Genesis 35:3 TLB.
6. Luke 11:9–10.
7. 2 Corinthians 12:7–10 ESV.

Day 49: Do You Have a "Shadow"?

1. Mark 1:33.
2. Mark 2:4.
3. Angela Lunde, "Fear Drives Shadowing of Alzheimer's Caregivers," Alzheimer's Blog, May 17, 2011. http://www.mayoclinic.org/diseases-conditions/alzheimers-disease/expert-blog/shadowing-and-alzheimers/bgp-20055944.

Day 50: Anchored

1. Matthew Henry's Commentary, Hebrews 6:19.
2. F. W. Farrar, Commentary on Hebrews 6, verse 19. Cambridge Bible for Schools and Colleges, Cambridge University Press, 1891.

Day 51: God's Opportunity
1. John chapter 9.
2. C. H. P., "February 23," *Streams in the Desert* (Grand Rapids: Zondervan, 1982), 61.

Day 53: The Spirit Prays for You
1. Mrs. Charles E. Cowman (compiler), "October 31," *Streams in the Desert* (Grand Rapids: Zondervan, 1982), 315.

Day 54: Hesed: God's Faithful Love
1. Hosea 6:6 NIV.
2. Lamentations 3:22.
3. 2 Samuel 9:7 NIV.
4. Ruth 1:8 NIV.
5. Iain Duguid, "Loyal-Love (Hesed)," *Tabletalk* magazine, http://www.ligonier.org/learn/articles/loyal-love-hesed/.

Day 56: Temptation
1. Genesis 2:24 ESV.
2. Deuteronomy 5:18.

Day 57: One
1. Luke 15:4–7 CSB.
2. John 3:1–18.
3. John 4:1–29.
4. Luke 19:1–10.
5. John 19:26–27.
6. Luke 23:43.
7. Matthew chapters 8 and 9.

Day 58: Silver Lining
1. C. S. Lewis, *The Problem of Pain*, revised edition (New York: Harper One, 2015).

Day 59: Worry
1. Tim Keller, Twitter post, May 3, 2012, 4:10 a.m., https://twitter.com/dailykeller/status/198006621262188544?lang=en.

Acknowledgments

I am grateful to the Lord for His guidance as I wrote these devotionals. I'm also very thankful for the friends who cheered me on and joined me in this writing adventure through their prayers. Big thanks go to my special encouragers, Jeannie Yarbrough and Anne Wagner.

I am especially grateful for the four spouse caregivers who each read and commented on a portion of the manuscript: Mary Hotvedt, Marcia Rogers, Patsy Justice, and Nancy Gray. Thank you, ladies, for sharing from your hearts and from your experience. I also want to thank my son, Chris Barr, for his helpful suggestions and Dr. Ed Shaw and Dr. Gary Chapman for their support and encouragement.

Last, but definitely not least, extra-special thanks go to Dwight Harris, who read all sixty devotionals, shared wonderful ideas and feedback, and encouraged me every single day. Dwight, you are the best! This devotional is lovingly and gratefully dedicated to you.

About the Author

Debbie Barr is a versatile writer and engaging speaker. *Grace for the Unexpected Journey,* her fifth book, was written with heartfelt compassion and admiration for Christian caregivers walking the dementia journey with a loved one.

A native of Berwick, Pennsylvania, Debbie now lives in Winston-Salem, North Carolina. You can read more about Debbie and see her other books at debbiebarr.com.

ALSO BY DEBORAH BARR

ANOTHER RESOURCE FOR ALZHEIMER'S
AND DEMENTIA CAREGIVERS

KEEPING
LOVE ALIVE
AS
MEMORIES
FADE

*The 5 Love Languages® and
the Alzheimer's Journey*

Deborah Barr, MA · Edward G. Shaw, MD
GARY CHAPMAN, PhD
#1 New York Times bestselling author of The 5 Love Languages®

978-0-8024-1450-2

"Through stories that are moving
and unflinching, *Keeping Love
Alive as Memories Fade* shows how
love can persist even as dementia
gradually erodes memory and
physical abilities. It offers
powerful testimony to the lasting
nature and immense power of
human relationships."

—PETER V. RABINS, MD, MPH
coauthor, *The 36-Hour Day*

NORTHFIELD
PUBLISHING